T0162371

THE
FUGITIVE
SELF

THE
FUGITIVE
SELF

New and Selected Poems by

John Wheatcroft

etruscan press

Etruscan Press
Wilkes University
84 West South Street
Wilkes-Barre, PA 18766

 WILKES UNIVERSITY

www.etruscanpress.org

Printed in the United States of America

Publishers Cataloging-in-Publication

Wheatcroft, John, 1925–
        The fugitive self : new and selected poems / John Wheatcroft. — 1st ed.
        p.   cm.
        Poems.
        ISBN-13: 978-0-9797450-9-6
        ISBN-10: 0-9797450-9-8
        I. Title.
        PS3573.H4F84 2009   813'.54
                                                   QBI09-600079

First Edition

Designed by Nicole DePolo

Cover image: *SkylineArc* © 2001 by Sharon Bowar, www.sharonbowar.com

Etruscan Press is committed to sustainability and environmental stewardship. We elected to
print this title through Bookmobile on FSC paper that contains 30% post consumer fiber
manufactured using biogas energy and 100% wind power.

Etruscan Press is grateful for the support from the
Stephen & Jeryl Oristaglio Foundation, Wilkes University,
Youngstown State University, NEOMFA, Nin & James Andrews Foundation,
Wean Foundation, Bates-Manzano Fund, and the
Council of Literary Magazines and Presses.

The Etruscan Press publication of the present edition
of *The Fugitive Self* has been made possible by a grant from the National
Endowment for the Arts.

NATIONAL
ENDOWMENT
FOR THE ARTS
A great nation
deserves great art.

Etruscan Press is a 501(c)(3) nonprofit organization.
Contributions to Etruscan Press are tax deductible
as allowed under applicable law.
For more information, a prospectus, or to order one of our titles,
contact us at etruscanpress@gmail.com.

BOOKS BY JOHN WHEATCROFT

POETRY
Death of a Clown
Prodigal Son
A Voice from the Hump
Ordering Demons
The Stare on the Donkey's Face
Random Necessities
Gowpen: A Double Handful of Poems
       with Karl Patten (limited edition)
Declaring Generations
       with Peter Balakian (limited edition)

FICTION
Edie Tells: A Portrait of the Artist as a Middle-aged Cleaning Woman
Catherine, Her Book
The Beholder's Eye
Killer Swan
Mother of All Loves
Trio with Four Players
The Education of Malcolm Palmer
Answering Fire
Slow Exposures

DRAMA
A Fourteenth-Century Poet's Vision of Christ:
      A poetic drama for voices and instruments,
      Music by Thomas Beversdorf
Ofoti

INTERVIEWS (editor)
Our Other Voices: Nine Poets Speaking

To Jack Stadler

and in memory of Thomas Yoseloff

ACKNOWLEDGMENTS

Grateful acknowledgment is made to A. S. Barnes & Co.,
Cornwall Books, Thomas Yoseloff, Ltd., and Associated
University Presses for permission to reprint poems from *Death
of a Clown*, 1964; *Prodigal Son*, 1967; *A Voice from the Hump*,
1977; *Ordering Demons*, 1981; *The Stare on the Donkey's Face*, 1990;
Random Necessities, 1999; also to the following publications
in which many of the poems in this volume, a number of
them under other titles and in slightly different versions, have
previously appeared: *Apostrophe, Approach, Ararat, Artful Dodge, The
Beachcomber, The Beloit Poetry Journal, Blue Guitar, The Carleton Miscellany,
The Carolina Quarterly, Cat's Ear, Denver Quarterly, Connecticut River
Review, The Dalhousie Review* (Canada), *Epoch, Forum, Four Quarters,
Garret, Graham House Review, The Humanist, The Husk, Illuminations,
Interim, The Literary Review, Main Street Rag, The Minnesota Review,
Nebo, Pennine Platform* (West Yorkshire, England), *Philadelphia
Poets, Poem, Red Rock Review, Seriously Meeting Karl Shapiro, Sidewalk*
(Edinburgh, Scotland), *South and West, South Dakota Review, The
Stepladder, The Wallace Stevens Journal, West Branch, Yarrow.*

"Alfresco" was published as a chapbook by The Press of
Appletree Alley, Lewisburg, PA 1995.

"De Mowbray's Men Re-Consecrate a Church" and
"Runagate" were published in *Declaring Generations,* with
Peter Balakian, a limited edition fine book, by The Press of
Appletree Alley, Lewisburg, PA, 1982.

"Emily Dickinson" was published in *Emily Dickinson: Letters
from the World,* The Cymric Press, Corinth, NY, 1970.

"I Know an Old Crone" was published under the title
"Sonnet" in *The New York Times,* 1961.

"Love and War" was published in *Seriously Meeting Karl Shapiro*, Negative Capability Press, Mobile, AL, 1993.

"Once by Seaside" was published in *Mademoiselle*, 1969.

"Oysters" was published in *From Mt. San Angelo*, The Virginia Center for the Creative Arts: Associated University Presses, Sweet Briar, VA, 1984.

"Rachel on Long Island Sand Dune" was published in *Harper's Bazaar*, 1963.

"The Second-Best Hotel in Chambery," was published in *The New York Times Book Review*, 1990.

Yaddo, the MacDowell Colony, and The Virginia Center for the Creative Arts provided hospitable places and the necessary time in which many of these poems were written. I am most appreciative.

For their judgment and suggestions I am deeply grateful to Peter Balakian, Philip Brady, Thomas Gardner, Bruce Smith, and Doris Umbers.

I am also deeply grateful to David Fletcher and John Murphy for the expert and generous help they provided in the preparation of the manuscript of this book.

CONTENTS

from *THE STARE ON THE DONKEY'S FACE*
1990

from *ORDERING DEMONS*
1981

iv

from *DEATH OF A CLOWN*
1964

Introduction

It is a great gift to be able to read John Wheatcroft's thirty-six new poems alongside this generous selection drawn from six earlier books. What one realizes, after spending time with them and allowing earlier and later poems to speak to each other across a lifetime of writing, is how many occur in a kind of charged, suspended place—the poet waking to himself "restless between two points of rest" ("Hitting a Pheasant on the Pennsylvania Turnpike"). That space between takes many forms. It is the space between war and home, as in the striking "Love and War." It is the space between a fading past and a dawn yet to come; between embracing and losing a parent; between belief and skepticism, the weight of history and the release of sleep. It is what one poem calls "a parenthesis in the dark," echoing the Anglo Saxon poem and describing a moment of love as "a sparrow's flight / through a great hall where / fire blazes on a winter night"—night and dark on either side of the flight. It is life itself, focused and unresolved.

What the speakers of these poems find themselves doing there—driving in the fog, remembering the century's horrors, shimming a tilting soul, making love—is trying to overcome a sense of division. It is as if one's identity, one's real identity, becomes clear in these spaces where one finds oneself naked or without an identity, suspended on barbed wire, powerless. Typically, Wheatcroft's speakers find themselves staring at an image in a cracked mirror, or witnessing the doubled play of lamp and firelight breaking a reflected face into chasms and fissures. They pause in a roadhouse on Christmas Eve, consumed by worry, far from home, distracted by a barmaid, and acknowledge themselves as divided, certain only that "lust and grief won't mix." They turn to lovers, attempting to wear away that sense of division, knowing full well that despite all of love's voices, "cherub coos, animal groans, demon sobs," "The music we make will break our hearts / without providing us / a glimmer of light in the dark."

It's finally that heartbreaking music that I most prize about these poems. Their sound is utterly distinctive: a slow, thick, deeply-stressed pressing forward, thrusting deeper, like a runner against a gale; and then a sudden racing ahead when the wind shifts and the voice is released to soar and sing and touch; once, and again, and then silence. As the volume's powerful title poem demonstrates, what's heartbreaking about this music is its deep commitment to finding again what would make it whole. In that poem, it's the uncanny memory of two souls merging ("I then and there became him") when a rival soldier, helplessly floating down through the air moments after being intent on bringing fiery death, is torn to bits by a barrage of shells. The music breaks your heart because it is never resolved; that unlooked-for bonding is never repeated. What would make the self whole remains always fugitive, always at large:

> To think, I've never known the name
> nor seen the face of the only other self
> I'm certain of. Still searching.

But the music of that search—probing, thinking, marveling; relentlessly sucked back, clawing its way forward—is the music of our time, here brilliantly and individually rendered.

— Tom Gardner

NEW POEMS

REPLY TO A PERSONAL

Dear Beautiful Soul,

I do solemnly swear
what you read is what you get.

Spineless as a jellyfish,
I take more shapes than water,
writhe like a python, have
more selves than the Trinity.

With nothing to hold onto
I clench my fists. Almost
down and out, I can't go back
or ahead. Struggling to stand
on my own two feet,
I constantly waver.

Because I refuse to pick up
the pieces of the past,
I can't map out a future.
With no promises to keep,
I don't know what I'm waiting for.

Too stiff-necked to hang my head,
I'm ashamed to hold it up.
When I plop it on a pillow,
I wrestle against myself,
dark angel I can't pin down.

The nightmare I wake up to
is crazier than my dreams.
As for love, it's a wag without a tale.

In an instant of letting go,
Dad and Mom misconceived.
Since they've tucked in their toes,
I've been trying to forgive them.
Dad bequeathed no mansions,
Mom can't intercede from the grave.

My days are strings of words
ending in Gordian knots.
Crooked my lines, my pages
ungathered, and the book
of me is unbound. Want me?

ON BORROWED TIME

As a sapling I might have blazed up
and burned out like the pine
my father put a match to
each twelfth day after Christmas,
I with a scarlet throat,
blood at the boiling point.
The doctor knew how much
depended on a red wheel barrow
my mother invoked as God.

A decade later my gut
was cut open. A grenade,
about to explode and make mincemeat
of my vitals, was forceped out
just in the nick of time.

Day two at Okinawa. I catch
a glimpse of the mask and goggles
inside the Plexiglas nose
of the Zero zeroing in on us,
on me! Seconds before
he'd have taken me with him,
willing his death for mine,
a five-inch shell translates
him to debris. It's for me
to ponder the life he'd given up.

For all the time I've borrowed,
the return on my sum is scant.
Whatever I've put my hand to
bears a ghostly thumbprint.

When the banker who holds all mortgages
calls in my loan, on what grounds
can I plead for a period of grace?

NIGHT MUSIC AFTER LA BELLE EPOQUE

i
Inside a green kimono
you lying stretched on a sofa,
your titian hair cascading
over a lavender pillow.

In the fireplace flames,
improvising a ballet
to Franck's *Sonata in A Major,*
which I've put on our old-fashioned phonograph,
light this otherwise dark room.
Only the music and sizzle, pop, crackle
of boiling sap break the silence.

So deep the dark beyond
the withdrawn draperies,
the moon must have tumbled
into a black hole in space.
Every single star
has burned itself out.
To the east of the house
beyond the terrace, lies
brackish Currituck Sound.

Seven bloody years
into the twenty-first century,
generations after the wars
to end all wars and usher
in peace have been fought and lost,
the killing still goes on.
We're caged in a darkening age.

ii
In the window on the west side of the house
my eye all at once picks up a lustrous pearl,
the tip of an invisible pointer,
gliding across the blackness
beyond the trinity of panes.
With a blink it slithers past a mullion
into the second panel of glass,
then into the third,
at which point or instant
(here now space is time and time is space)
a glowing ruby enters the dark first pane,
and trails its pearly forerunner
at a constant distance.

As the bead of red
slides into the second pane,
the pearl disappears.
Seconds later the ruby is also gone.

Were I to ask you whence
these mysterious spots of color,
moving in the darkness that envelopes us,
you'd reply, oh, the neighbor who lives
beyond us in this cul-de-sac
has just returned from somewhere.

While the fact of him in his black Corvette
is certain as my self is in my body,
it misses the point of my question.

iii
Marcel Proust purloined "a little phrase,"
only five notes, which I hope, believe, imagine
I just have heard, from Franck's *Sonata*
and smuggled it into the music
of one M. Vinteuil, who composes
only in Proust's true fiction.

For Marcel's Swann, whose lover
has just betrayed him, to hear again
the five-note melody is the instant
"at the beginning of the world as if
there were none but these two on earth."
For us might it turn out to be
the instant at the end?

iv
When the fire has burned itself to ash
and the phonograph has gone silent,
we'll retreat to the refuge of bed.
In "that great black impenetrable night,"
which Marcel feared and lusted after,
you'll be the fine-tuned strings,
I the thrusting bow.
The music we make will break our hearts
without providing us
a glimmer of light in the dark.

WAITING

Nothing we'd been counting on
all the time we'd waited
was waiting when we arrived.

Only more waiting—
for waves to cease surging to mountains
restlessly overthrowing themselves,
aeons of geology in seconds,

waiting during the hush
after the smack of swell
on sand, followed by the suck
of withdrawal before
the next upheaval,

waiting for wind to quit
lashing palm fronds, penitents
hissing pain as they danced,

waiting for heaven's spigots to close,
to end the pitipat pitipat pitipat
on the orange pantile roof,
echoing inside our head.

And the dogs of night, aroused
by the chaos of water and wind—
we waited for them to lose heart
and voice, and give in to sleep.

Oh yes, during this time so precious
to us who'd come so far
to escape the dominion of ice,
we were waiting for a sign,
a sea change that never came
in the days allotted in this place
that had been sold to us as paradise:

for a bird with a leaf in its beak to
alight on the veranda,
for a rainbow to bend over a sea
lulled gentle by sighs of breeze…

for sun to sponge up the murk,
for stars to display themselves
in patterns we'd never seen,
for stillness to hush the hubbub.

*

All the way home, with nothing
to show for going, we waited—
for what? Something, anything.

You'd think by then we'd have learned
to winnow wanting from waiting,
would have prepared ourselves for
the void awaiting our return.

Over and over we relive the waiting
of whatever we were before we conceived
the sense to know we were waiting—
the egg waiting to be wooed,
the sperm waiting for welcome,
the cell their wedding begets
waiting to multiply.

Then waiting to come to term,
when the sac, our Ur-home, bursts,
anoints constricting walls
and launches us down the slippery slope,

where we wait to pop out,
a glob from a toothpaste tube,
our first locomotion
into a world of waiting.

*

What does it matter or mean,
chafing or submitting, riding
on hope or squatting in despair,
staying put now, going where when,
coming back then,

since all our waiting is
for the permanence of absence,
the sameness of space,
the absolute of silence,
the fulfillment of naught?

THE SOUL CHANGER

> Most men are in the course of their lives
> frequently unlike themselves, and even
> seem to be transformed into others, very
> different from what they were.
>   —Rousseau, *The Confessions*

i

For every given body there are seven souls,
the opposite of crustaceans
with their multiple carapaces.
It's the soul changer's function
to remove an exhausted soul and replace
it with a fresh one while the body's sleeping.
His touch is delicate beyond all instruments,
the procedure, painless.

When the body awakens the morning after,
it has no knowledge soul surgery
has been performed.

ii

Most bodies can recall their most recent souls.
When more than three or four intervene, old souls
frequently seem strange as the face in a faded photograph
with your name on the back. Those who do
remember their earlier souls often disown them.

Traces of forgotten and disavowed souls,
montaged, broken, disfigured,
flit through dreams, sleeping and waking.

Unlike money, souls can't be loaned,
borrowed, given away or stolen.
They're not transplantable as are kidneys,
livers and hearts. One of a kind,
a soul must be accepted in the order ordained.

Souls are not embedded, as are teeth and brains,
nor attached with hinges, like bones.
They are dispersed throughout the body
in an intricate web of pulse-strings
that can't be weighed or measured.
Without color or shadow, they're impervious
to x-rays, scans and MRIs.

iv
Sometimes the soul changer gets bored with his work
and nods. Then he might insert
an inappropriate soul—
an ugly into a beautiful body,
a chaste into a promiscuous, etc.,
or retire a soul before its time is up.

He's been known to cram two souls
that are incompatible into a single body.
On occasion he's failed to notice a soul
is dying to be superseded
or has already died. For a body
to carry on when its soul is dead
is no laughing matter. The results
of the soul changers' slip-ups
are hilariously painful.

Blessed be those bodies that fail to outlive
their birth soul. Like animals, they enjoy
one soul that lasts a lifetime.

The soul changer has no jurisdiction
over beasts, fish, fowl, or insects.

Some who endure aspire to sainthood,
deluding themselves and the world into believing,
no matter the number of souls they've run through,
they're virgin-souled, exempt
from the soul changer's office.
Having lived through three or four changes,
most find the game's not worth the candle.

vi
Few bodies hang on long enough
to use their full allotment.
It's the rarest of rares that a body's allowed
to give up the ghost at the instant
soul number seven is spent. The process
is timed so whole and fragments of souls
will be left over. Unused souls and hunks
of souls abound. Woe to the body
that outlasts its seventh soul.

Worn-out souls cannot be reconditioned
or repaired, as can the things of this world.
Nor can parts or superfluous souls be put to use.
Soul changing is not an efficient operation.

vii
The soul changer's source of supply
is unknown. His dumping ground
is the bottomless pit of forever.

All humankind are birthright members
of the Congregation of Seven Souls.

SONG OF THE ALHAMBRA

> Give him alms, give him alms,
> for in life there is nothing like
> the heartache of blindness in Granada.
> —Francisco de Icaza

Boabdil, the valiant Moor, blubbered
like a baby after losing it to
"the Catholic Kings." To fumigate
the stench of burning Jews, the angels
of Columbus beguiled themselves
among the lilies here. Their grandson,
Charles the Fifth, neither holy nor Roman
emperor, debauched in its grandeur.

The Alhambra's layered beauties are
the only signatures of generations
of artists, artisans and slaves who wrought it.
Their names should be inscribed
indelibly in blood.

As I shamble from the last lush garden,
purblind from looking,
my ear is taken by a voice
whose words I can't make out.
It's sweet enough to melt a hangman's heart.

Tracking the chant to a niche,
in which a prophet or a saint might repose,
I light on two bulging milky eyes
in the face of a very dark
and very small and very ancient man.

Squatting on a tripod stool, he's sandwiched
between two boards that blazon tickets
whose reds, blues, purples, golds, and greens
only his fingers know.

Doubting there is a winning number,
I pay double for a gold.

SOAKING IN HISTORY

Impregnable Carcassonne,
la Vierge de Languedoc,
with steep and cobbled streets,
is no place for tender soles or hearts.

Lolling in a tub in a marble bath,
I'm up to my neck in Laodicean water.
With no more will than stone,
I'm immersed in history.

Visigoths, Romans, Gauls,
Franks, Moors, and Albigensians,
gouged, levered, hoisted, chiseled
this hump on earth's backbone.
To make this stronghold, take and keep it,
they covered the scar with blood.

I think of English Edward's darling boy,
destined not to be the Fourth,
in midnight armor, on a pitch-black charger,
coming on this rock. Finding it all
it was cracked up to be, he saved
his princely face, served God
and his father too, by slaughtering
innocents outside the moated wall.

The tub contains me like a sarcophagus.
And I picture Jean Marat, submerged
in his *baquet,* to assuage the itch
he'd caught hiding in Paris sewers.

Gnawing beneath his skin, it was driving
him mad. When Charlotte Corday cured
him with a knife, water turned to wine.

Complacencies of the *baignoire*.
Somehow an empress' bathtub landed
on Grenada, of all outlandish places.
To think, inflated with hope, Napoleon
seeded the body that herein languished.
Oh, Marie, Josèphe Rose Tascher
de La Pagerie Beauharnais!
with all your beauty and passion
you came up empty.

In veins of gray-black marble between the faucets
of the tub, I trace a face on a bull neck bound
by an iron collar. The head is bowed
in defiance or submission.

An idler in this tourist trap hotel,
who am I to adjudicate
the echoing claims of the dead?
Recusing myself, I scissor the plug
between two toes and worm it free.
As water swirls down the drain.
my naked self emerges.
When the plumbing burps *fini,*
I climb from the tub and robe myself in terry.

No conqueror or conquered,
nor murderer or martyr,
neither master nor slave,
a disarmed man in the middle,
I shamble off.

Beyond this citadel lies history
in the making—brutal, bloody, bootless.
How small the soak has shrunk me.

UNAUTHORIZED VERSION

Never looking up or around,
the man husbanded ground-food—
mast, truffles, taro, beetroot.
He took her as he plucked
a low-hanging fig or date.

Bored, she began to look
beyond, above, askance.
One day a creature of a kind
she'd never seen before,
twisted around a branch
of a tree, whose leaves flamed scarlet,
which she had never noticed,
bowed his diamond head,
blue-green, sparkling in sunlight,
then whispered in her ear,
"Sweet, sweet, sweet."
Such gallantry bowled her over.

Innocent the doing. Not so
re-doing in her mind.
Knowing changed it all.

Confessed to, he wondered why
she was making such a thing of it.
On he went, in the old way,
stolidly, sweating in daylight,
work-weary in the dark.
Hearing him belch once during,
she realized he was vulgar.

As the infant sucked her dugs,
fat with memory's whey,
upturned with desire's curd,
his ugliness made her weep.
Istor, she named him, her knowingness.
All night he howled with colic.
As he grew, she pampered him.

A second son was daddy's boy.
One day at play the first-born knocked
the younger's brains out with a rock.
The old man kicked him out.

Before they went to seed,
they sowed another crop.

Banding against the outcast,
the junior brothers collared him,
covered his parts with a pelt,
and chained him to a stake.

More civilized, their children
undertook to tame him,
cropping his hair, clipping
his horny nails, and clothing
him decently in stammel.
He never seemed to age.

Finding the things of this world
easy to grasp, he proved
to be dexterous with tools—
bending bows, whittling arrows,
forging swords, spears, shields,
delving holes for corpses,
setting ridgepoles, thatching

roofs, buttressing walls.
Able to fathom forces,
he contained them in an arch.

When the cathedral they'd appointed
him to raise was finished,
he displayed his old brass collar
in a showcase. Everyone
wanted the relic. He auctioned
it off for a pretty penny.

Quitting labor, he dressed
himself in finery, changed his name,
wedded a magistrate's daughter.
Poets began embroidering his story.

THE OTHER SIDE OF THE STORY

Beside me, so close we could hold hands
if it weren't for the nails,
hangs a local whacko and rabble-rouser,
who, with a handful of hangers on,
has been stirring up multitudes in these parts
with promises of heaven on earth,
here and now, with no Romans or Sadducees
to rag us. He claims he can cure
all sicknesses, including Venus' curse,
fix any fault, is even able to bring
the dead to life. And the mob believes him.

Well, his sugary tongue got caught between the teeth of
the powers that be. "Just nuisance," declared
the governor, figuring a lunatic
wasn't a threat to swords and spears,
shields and helmets. Not worth the price
of the nails. "Dangerously guilty!"
the high priest pronounced, fearful
that turning on the rabble might knock
the props from under the stony laws
that let him lord it over us poor riffraff.

Though the Roman washed his hands of it, he let
the spectacle go on. Nabbed carrying off
a lamb when the moon was high and bright,
it was just my luck to be made a part of the sideshow.

To get a laugh from the crowd, the toadies
of some Levite have crowned
the crack-brained rube with thorns

and scrawled a sign above his head
proclaiming him the king we haven't got.

On the other side of the "king," hangs one
of my sort, who I can hear without being able
to see. Listening to him spill his guts
and whimper how sorry he is for all the sheep
he's snatched and wishes he could give them back
would make me vomit if anything was left
to spew. Having his number, I know
what he's really sorry about is getting caught.

Now the nut case is forgiving him,
as if he was one of Caesar's judges,
promising him a place in paradise.
If such a place existed, it would
only be for all the bastards that run
this rotten world we're in and make
the likes of us steal sheep to keep
the old ones and our women and kids from starving.

Maybe the two I'm hanging with
are counting on a miracle—
the sun to stand still, earth shake and quake,
graves open, and corpses, good and bad,
holy and wicked, innocent and guilty,
come back to life, though why
they'd ever want to is beyond me.

All that's donkey shit. If a miracle
could happen, I suppose the nails would fall
out of six hands and feet, and blood would run
backward into veins. Well, let me tell you, nails
are nails and blood pours out like water when

the pot is full of holes and flesh is for
the birds—hawks, vultures, and ravens.
Believe me, we go dried-out, picked clean to the bone.

I look down on the madman's mama,
she has to be, and a long-haired babe,
maybe his bimbo—after all, he's human.
In front of the crowd at his feet,
they're hugging each other and blubbering.

If she weren't long gone, the mother I
remember knocking me around as a kid
wouldn't be caught dead here, I can tell you.
And my woman's already found another man,
a piece of sunshine I was given
while waiting in the dungeon to climb the hill.

You can bet as many years as you
have left against a lonely death
that none of the sniveler's blood-sworn pals
or any who followed the miracle man
have showed up for the main event.
For me, no tears, no grief, no mourning.
Whatever I did, I did solo. And so I go.

Minutes that seem like hours ago
I gave up my final howl of pain.
Knowing I'm running out of blood—
really it's running out of me—
I've sealed my lips, and swallowed,
without choking on, all the wrongs
that were done me and that made me do
all that I did. Both are hid in my gut
and there they will be buried.

Now the worst of it is finished.
Though the darkness coming on while the sun
is scorching tells me my mind will soon be gone,
I know enough to know I've no regrets
and feel no shame for doing what I had to,
also enough to know I never cringed.

NATIVITY QUINTET

i A Merchant's Tale

It may be as you say—each star
is fixed forever in the heavens.
Yet hear what these eyes of mine once saw.

I was in my third decade
and Cyrenius was Syria's governor.
The Roman Caesar had decreed
each man be taxed at his birthplace.
On the road from Damascus to Joppa
with a load of wool cloth,
I stopped on the third night to rest.
It was no caravansary but a little inn
where a merchant like me wouldn't be robbed
or cheated too much. So many had come
to be taxed, the landlord had no room,
just a space beneath the roof
in which I could throw down a pallet.
Removing my headdress and washing the sweat
from my face, the sand from my feet,
I went out to care for my donkey,
a contrary little beast,
but strong—my livelihood.

At the stable door I heard groaning
and was able to see, in the dusky light,
from a small oil lamp, a woman
lying in straw and worse, on the earthen floor.
At that very instant a burst of light
directly above the stable turned
midnight to noon. It made me blink.

A star would have had to come loose,
if stars are fixed as you claim.
As it stood blazing above me
I thought, I must be dreaming.
Some shepherds tending their sheep
in a pasture beside the inn
fell to their knees and chanted strange songs,
to their god I suppose. There came a great clap
of thunder too, I remember.

When I stumbled into the stable,
a man was just laying a new-born babe
in the trough with feed for my donkey.
What a chill was on the night!
I still can't tell you what made me,
tight-fisted fellow I've had to be
to get by, tear off a tag end of cloth
from one of the bundles still
in the panniers on the back of my donkey.
It barely covered the baby.
The mother smiled a faint smile.

Marking me as a Syrian,
the father shook his head.
"Kind sir, I have nothing to pay."
"A gift for the child," I muttered,
untying my donkey's burden,
then feeding him by hand.
"May it bring him the luck he'll need
on this thorny earth of ours."

Betimes I've wondered what's been
the chance of that child, who today
would be the age I was at his birth.

The story I've told you, my learned friend,
is not moonshine on the desert. That night
these eyes, now blind, saw a star break loose
in the sky and light up the world.

ii. Adoration of the Donkey: A Song Without Words

Lady, lying on earth
littered with straw and such
as we beasts let drop,
I see in your face the joy
release from a burden brings.

While my master was tethering me
to a post beside this shed,
a blaze of light from a star
made a brilliant flash in the darkness.
Did you squeeze your eyes against it,
as I did mine? Strange sounds
streaming down from the sky
made me prick up my pointed ears
and lift my fat lips from the water tub
though my tongue was swollen with thirst.

Lady, let the feed trough
here in the stable serve
as a crib for the baby you've birthed.
Don't worry, I'll be fed
from the granary by the hand
of my master, whose heart is soft
as ewe's wool, though his tongue
can be rough as sand. When he's cross
or angry or worried and tells me
I'm only a stupid ass,
I shake my head and bray,
and stamp my left forefoot.

I'd never kick him, though,
because he never beats me
as masters do their donkeys.
Look, now he's tearing a length
of cloth from one of the panniers
on my back. It's wool for haggling
over by the span in the market
dockside in far-off Joppa.

A donkey is born to complain.
But the weighty truth is this load
I've been bearing from Damascus
has grown heavier with each step.
Yet, lady, I swear to you,
the instant my master spread
the cloth over your child
to ward off night's chill, my burden
turned light as a handful of grain.

Now the halter's gone from my neck,
and my donkey's heart knows joy—
as if I've been led from this wasteland the gods
forgot to a pasture green, with warm,
not scorching sunlight, beside still water.

Lady, should danger threaten
you, if I could I'd carry you
and the little one there
to a land where you'd be safe,
far as the place might be.
When your child has reached manhood
may his fate not be a merchant's,
who must be rough to survive.
Let the gods make him a prince,
loving-kind to all people and
gentle to beasts of burden.

And, lady, you have my promise,
should the buzzards that scour the desert
not have picked me to the bone,
I'd bear your royal son
among waving palms and shouts
through the gates of some great city,
I not an Assyrian warhorse,
only a poor dumb donkey.

iii. Thief at the Nativity

This night these hills are cold.
Fine weather for the bold.

While shepherds lie wrapped in sleep,
I'll have myself a sheep.

With a big-bellied wife to feed,
God knows, I have great need.

"Cheer, dame," I'll chirk, "here's meat
for you and our spawn to eat,"

—adding another jot
against our 'thou shall not...'

The poor must risk being damned,
says Moses' eighth command.

Break Caesar's law I could
find myself spiked to wood.

*

As I climb the slope a light
makes morning out of night,

and sound bursts from the sky
near where the shepherds lie.

Before my chance to take
a sheep, they've come awake

and deem me one of them
when I say, "From Bethlehem,"

in answer to "Whence come you?"
"I've found a straggling ewe,"

I purr, as I twiddle the stray
I'd fixed on for my prey.

"Good sir, how kind you are.
But, look, a falling star...

no! lightning's struck the stable.
Hurry, we may be able

to help put out the blaze,
while sheep here safely graze."

We find no fire. Instead,
in a trough within a shed

beside the inn, a lady
has laid her new-born baby.

A Syrian trader hacks
from a pack on his donkey's back

a tag end of some wool.
Astonished, I watch him pull

it over the child. A man
in the shadows sighs, "We can,

alas, pay nothing, sir."
The child's sire but not her

husband is my shrewd guess.
"All we can do is bless

you to our Father." "Phaugh,
it's nothing. The night is raw,

and wind blows cold and wild
on these hills. Too soon the child

for itself will discover what
is every creature's lot,"

the Syrian growls, as he feeds
his beast by hand. No sheep

have I the heart to steal
this night. Dear God, a meal

for kites is the end I see
for me nailed on a tree.

And will my life be spent
before I can repent?

iv. Fathering

So many sons of David have gathered
at Bethlehem to pay great Caesar's tax
that the inn overflows. Pitying the woman's travail

on this chill and moonless night,
the landlord has sheltered us in this stable.

As she delivered the child into my hands,
bloodying them, her moaning rose
to a cry, either of pain or joy,
then subsided to low sobs. I heard
her gasp the name of the Father
of us all. Light from a single great star
burst forth, making it day in the stable.
Outside, voices were singing a psalm
of rejoicing—shepherds' they must have been.
Delicately I laid the newborn in a crib.

A Syrian merchant came lumbering in,
to feed his donkey, burdened with bales.
As I stooped to remove her babe from the trough,
the Syrian held up his thick weathered hands
and shook his head. Then he tore a length
of wool cloth from one of his panniers
and spread it gently over the child.

"I fear I can pay you nothing, sir," I said
with shame and lowered my head. The floor
of the stable was covered with straw and dung.

"A gift for the child," the Syrian growled
as he commenced to feed his beast by hand.

Just as I had no cloth to cover him,
no coin to give the stranger for his kindness,
I've had no part in this child.
When, knowing me a lowly carpenter,
possessed of no lands or flocks, of an age
to be her father, she accepted my courtship,

I had to wonder whether like many a girl
these days, she sorely needed a husband.

It turned out as I'd feared. When her robe
could no longer hide her swelling belly,
she told me one night a visitor from on high
had appeared, that he'd blessed her, then revealed
that secretly the Heavenly One overshadowing her,
had fathered a child in her womb. Soon after
in a dream an angel required of me
to accept her publicly, without complaint
or harboring anger or show of shame.

As now I look at the child, warmed in a trough
under the cloth of a Syrian, the woman kneeling
on straw and droppings beside him, I know he's come
to this earth as pure as light from that star.

Whether these visions be false or true,
revealing the Holy Presence, I
will consider this child my own, raise him
as my son. So he can make his way in this world
of hardship, I'll teach him my trade,
all the uses of wood and hammer and nails.

v. Childbirth Song

Prickly with straw and covered
with dung, the floor of this stable
is the appointed place for the birth
of my child, in the chill of this night.

Between the pangs that began
as we'd found shelter here,
the sweet cool smell of rain

that had ended long drought,
the morning after the night
I'd been told I was with child,
came back. I took that scent
as a pledge a flower would
root and bloom in this desert.

I remembered too the flutter
I'd felt inside one day
during heat of the following season.
It told me that I was the bearer
of another heart that beat.

Now that my agony has begun
I recall that first kick from a foot
within me. By then my secret
had grown too great to be hid.

Somehow I knew the stir of that foot
was a sign that in his manhood
he would walk among the people,
would feel their hunger and pain,
would provide them bread and wine,
would give them comfort and heal them.

Oh! Something inside me breaks open.
As light from a star right above
this shed turns night to noon
I'm torn apart by love.
                        *
My man picks up the child
and lays him in the crib
where travelers' beasts are fed.
On the open side of the stable
herdsmen, whose sheep must graze

nearby, appear. As they
suddenly break into a song
of praise to our Creator,
I see a merchant approach.

Blinking at the brightness, he leads
his donkey, on whose back
two panniers bulge with cloth,
to the manger my baby lies in.

When he sees the father bend
to lift the child from the crib,
then a woman in childbed beneath,
he shakes his head. Though not
one of us, he tears a swatch
of wool from one of his bundles
and spreads it over my son

While the donkey is eating
from the hand of his master, my heart
knows a peace that no man can
understand and joy unbounded.

ACCOUNTING FOR ABSENCE

To Penelope

A ten-year struggle,
sometimes internecine.
Futile assaults on a citadel,
in which someone else's bride
primped and preened,
while we, her would-be rescuers, died.
Victory, when it came, was hollow as the horse
that contrived in one night
more than all those years of force.

This you have heard before.
Be patient, wife, and learn
the hazard of my return.

Lashed to my own ship's mast
while lured by ravishing voices;
promised a now that has no past
or future; trapped in a cave
and almost done in by mindless might
that I plunged into endless night;
bewitched by degrading love;
faced with two choices
with consequences equally grave;

dispatched to a land
where the dead are alive
but can't be touched; storm-tossed,
swamped, compelled to dive
and clutch a plank that let me alone survive;
having to swim for it; almost lost

in a vengeful sea;
washed up on a strand
where a people of benevolence,
practitioners of hospitality, provided me
a ship, manned by a crew of their own
flesh and blood, whose recompense
was to be turned to stone;

deposited asleep
on a shore I failed to recognize
as my island home
until a goddess, I swear, appeared
and instructed me to kiss
my native soil, making me weep
for joy. When the mist
clouding my mind had cleared,
the goddess disappeared.

Love, I'm telling you no lies:
I've wandered these ten years
in the wine-dark of your eyes.

Lear at Dover

A wily general, more soldier than
her husband, she bred occasion to unman me.
Repairing to her sister seeking shelter,
I met a storm of rage. Instead of the cordial
I'd been thirsting for, the third already
had tendered me a cup I took as bitters.
For that I disavowed her. The imp,
whose motley spares him, has stripped me naked.

It's taken the blinding of a cross-eyed father
who, scenting the spoor of my mortality,
has nosed his way to Dover, to make me see
the glint of knives I'd kept beneath
my pillow, the heart that's true, the clown
who's wise, the fool who's a once-was king.

LATIN LOVER

"Cis-e-row I sit in?" I,
deriding what's in store for us
in Latin Two, throw at Blinky Blinn
as we slouch into our seats.

Scorning my lame-tame humor,
Blink shoots back at me,
"If *principis* is the genitive of *princeps,*
what's the genitive of *takeps?*"
—proof that over the summer he's retained
the third declension gloomy Mr. Peckham
had drilled into our brains
as we'd tangled with the tactics
of *Caesar's Wars* in Latin One.

Before I can concoct an answer,
a buzzer announces the hour.
Slender, tall and stately as Minerva,
Miss Cavanaugh, her silver hair
swept back into a comb, with skin
that rivals nacre, glides through the door.
She greets, disarms and hushes us.
"Friends, countrymen, and students,
lend me your precious ears."

She was our cicerone
through the labyrinth clauses
within clauses within clauses
in *Oratio in Catilinam Prima.*
Stumped by periphrastic conjugations,
cringing before deponent verbs,
we, unlike Catiline, whose plots

exhausted Tully's patience,
never used up hers. No one
dared conspire in her classroom.

She made us hold our living tongues
while cherishing the dead one
she gave breath to. Her smile
and praxis taught us what
dulce et decorum really means.
I was sixteen. She, sixty-some,
became my secret love.

So many decades gone,
yet memory has enshrined Miss Cavanaugh
in an empyrean, where
her radiance outshines the faded luster
of all my Venus-loves.
Her given name was Margaret,
Latin for a pearl.

AN IRREVERENT MEDITATION ON THE END OF TIME

"To the last syllable of recorded time…"
the bombastic metaphor
of a fictitious king
facing his play-ending end?
Or does the poet-playwright
stand behind his figure?

Who records time? Why and where?
Who will utter the final syllable?
While doing what? When?
What will be its consequence?
Will it end all communication?
What will the last syllable be?
in Faeroese? Pashto? Gujarati?
Baluchi? Sindhi? English?
Unrecorded, will time then cease to be?

A poet who kept his eye on the elements
offered alternatives: fire or ice?
Some choice. Both lover and hater,
he wanted it both ways. Burned to a clinker
or frozen to an ice cube, will that syllable
be preserved as a memento mori
or annihilated to give some nonsyllabic
new creation a fresh beginning? Will God,
conceding failure, cease to utter?
His choir go dumb? Will Satan
give up on maledictions?

The wife of a priestly-solemn poet,
rather chilly too, deconstructed
her husband's gloomy eschatology.

When asked with whom she'd been abroad
on her return from having cut a caper
with a down-to-earth philosopher
on the incontinent Continent,
she let her tongue shoot back quick as
a striking cobra's: "Not with a wimp but a banger."

Time time time…poets conjure figures
dread and witty, physicists insist the yarn's
so warped it's possible—God forbid—
to make time travel backward.

Here in northern climes we've trumped
all metaphor with our practice.
Our ancestors, enduring sun's cold shoulder,
which lengthens winter, diminishing our days
and shortening growth for crops and hours
for productive labor, taught us time
is money and will be till the last
dollar of legal tender has been spent.

VARIATION ON A THEME OF WALLACE STEVENS'

Returning home late yesterday afternoon,
I found a yellow slip stuffed in my mailbox,
informing me an effort had been made
to deliver a package earlier in the day.
If I wished it to be left sometime tomorrow
with no one there to sign for it, I was
to put my signature below. I did.

There it was on the porch, still is—a carton the shape
of a huge cigar box or drawer of a dresser.
On the heavy paper it was securely wrapped in,
my name and address were printed in black ink.
The sender's name was nowhere to be seen.

To lift the box from the tailgate and lug it up
the walk, then drop it smack on my front doorstep
must have taken a muscular one. Finding the box
blocking my going out and coming in,
I've resorted to using the door at the back of the house.

Early this morning, day three it is, as I came
around to the front, I made myself stare at the box.
It shook, I swear it shook as if fierce wind
were blowing and the box were filled with dust
or nothingness, though the air was perfectly still.

At seven tomorrow morning, the scheduled time,
I'll be waiting in the drive to glad-hand and mutter
a few words in the ear of the boss who's sitting
behind the wheel of the trash collection truck,
with the stub of a big cigar between his teeth.
Resistant as he is for his brawny "boys"

to pick up what won't fit in the steel containers,
he'll find in his palm a sum sufficient to have
the box removed and fed to the compactor.

Despite its imminent disposal,
I feel uneasy about the great big crate
I never ordered.

WALLACE STEVENS' SWAN SONG

St. Francis Hospital
Hartford, Connecticut

Suppose there is a soul
and it has specific gravity.
Remember, the first saint,
in a moment of faithlessness
sank like a rock.

On my way to sea
I have water on the brain
and in the heart.
Oh, I've heard the song of the surf
and have given song back.

Imagine, going under grabbing for
a couple of crossed sticks.

OVER HIS DEAD BODY

Grass mats are stacked beside a mound
of earth. The walls of the hole look raw.

On one side stands a line of bareheaded men,
veiled women, and a woman who is hooded.

Across from them men in a line
wear yarmulkes, women plain black hats.

At the head of the box, each close to his people,
two bearded men are almost rubbing shoulders.
They've done all that their followers would allow.

At the foot of the box three men in tailcoats
and striped gray trousers, holding black fedoras
over their crotches, shift from foot to foot.
They're waiting to drop the box down into the hole.

Mutually silent grief is rent by a cry.
The hooded woman flings herself on the coffin,
begins to pound the lid with her little fists.

From the side of veils a man tiptoes behind
the bearded men to the side of yarmulkes.

"Our mother wishes to kiss her son this one last time,"
he whispers, lips to the ear of a woman who
clutches a child. "It's the custom of our people."

Eyes on the slabs of sod, the woman shakes
her head. "Tell her I'm sorry. We agreed

to keep the casket closed. Imagine what
opening it now would do to our innocent daughter."

A look from the brother entreats the bearded man
nearest to his kin, whose look appeals
to his counterpart, who looks toward the men
in tailcoats, whose stony stare declares
the matter lies in somebody else's office.

Clawing the lid of the coffin,
the mother begins to wail.

WOLVES

The packs gather in darkness.
Divesting themselves of manhood,
they're thirsting for the blood
of those of a different faith.

Red-eyed, they rampage through village
and town. With rock-hard paws
they pound on doors and howl.

Men who come out and confront them
they gore with bayonet teeth.
Doors bolted against them they batter
and shatter. They smell out women
and children, the old ones crouching
in attics, closets and cellars.
With grappling-iron claws they drag them
into alleys, streets and squares.
And the cobbles are painted red.

Come sunrise, not a trace can be found
of those who had kept their faith.
Silent homes stand witness.

Returned to their dens, the packs
assume the trappings of humanity
and go about their business.

In Time of Torment

Only those in the throes of torture know
how quickly they'd abjure their right to exist.
For disbelievers they have scars to show.

Unlike the lucky narcotized who go
gently into the night of their final tryst,
those who have been designated know

beneath black hoods they're free to howl while slow
death comes as they writhe, chained by ankles and wrists.
No "few bad apples" caused their scars to show—

from dogs' teeth, water boards, cigarette burns, blows
from rifle butts to the head, the leathery kiss
of a boot on the mouth. Forsaken by law, they know

their claims and appeals go unheard. The torturers owe
them nothing but pain. Their names won't appear on lists
of wounded, dead and missing. Scars that show

will melt with flesh. The Tigris still will flow,
the breath of tanks exhaust in sandy mists.
But those who winked, condoning torture, know
the scars they bear true history will show.

HANDS

All the bloody hands of all those children
decorate the limbs of sugar maples
on land our fathers thieved and called New Eden.

The brains and nerves of boys we've taught "humanities"
perform as at a party they would be dropping
clothespins in a bottle for a kiss.

We've jetted them to heights that show how far
our brain has lofted us from living earth,
how cold our blood can run when we're on high.

To *Kindermord* tack on the massacre
of beasts, whose eyes can't comprehend and wait
for nothing, the gratuity of slaughter.

Cries from halfway around the world dumbfound
love's tongue. By day I fumble letters, a child
bereft of hands presented with alphabet blocks.

And meditate on bats, whose webbed hands fly
them blind in darkness. They feed on unseen prey,
sleep hidden, hanging upside down, like traitors.

REFLECTION

It is and it isn't my father's face
I'm shaving while listening to the news.

Again the bombs are chastening,
the missiles redeeming. We regret
mistakes and conduct investigations.

George Herbert, who like my father
pastored sheep, asked, "My God,
what is a heart?" Matter, we mutter,
a mass of programmed matter.
What matters matter? "'Tis but
a man gone," a woman, a child.

Coming across my father down
on his knees when *il Duce*
plucked the Lion of Judah's beard,
again when *der Führer*, his pal,
shattered glass, the child I was was scared.

In the tangle of nerves between
my brain and heart, love's snared.
Killing's conscripted my pen.

FUGITIVE SELF

i
Never reflected in a mirror or still water
nor coaxed or baited by a nod or smile
to endure exposure to a camera's eye,
nor making an appearance in a dream.

Once, I think, in the cellar of
an abandoned house, in which I struck
a match and gasped. Fleeing or seeking?

Yet again, perhaps, sitting naked on a bedside,
alone, in a strange room, lured out of sleep
by that old trickster consciousness, wondering
why I was where I was at just that moment.

And I remember an instant during
midsummer drought, when desperate
enough to pray, or dance, for rain, I felt
myself embedded in the hill across
a dried-up stream, deep in the darkness and silence
of earth, tangled among the massive roots
of beech, ash, hickory, hackberry, ironwood,
grappling and sucking for water that was not there.
Till then I had never known the thirst that kills.

ii
About a sighting wars ago, I have
no escape-route doubt. Spotting, identifying
a plane in the twin-lensed circles of my binoculars,
tracking it as it approached, I duly
reported him as my enemy designate.

A salvo of tracer shells, blitzing like
a swarm of angry hornets from the hives
of our ack-ack guns, turned his plane to the hell
of a burning cross. Freeing himself somehow,
hanging in the harness of a parachute,
slowly he descended through an azure sky
toward the sea of peace.

His helplessness and hands-up posture
declared for him the war was over.

The barrage went on, shells tore into
his flowering youth, and scattered it all
to petals. I then and there became him.
Two souls merged in the body that survived.

To think, I've never known the name
nor seen the face of the only other self
I'm certain of. Still searching.

"THE READINESS IS ALL"
—Hamlet

Drowsing in a rocker while
she waited, she tuned her ear
to voices long gone silent.
When the taxicab she'd phoned
for came, she failed to hear
the door chime, the fist-knock
on the glass, the driver shout,
"Hey, did anybody here call a cab?"

A hoodlum lurking on the street
saw the taxi drive away
without its passenger.
Finding her door unlocked,
he went skulking in,
snapped her cane in half,
smashed her glasses, ground
his heel on her hearing aid,
and just for the hell of it,
beat her black and blue.

Bedfast now, she drools and dribbles.
In her eyes we read a plea:
please call another cab.
Whatever the meter reads
I'll pay double and tip the driver
all that I have left. For God's sake
call another cab. Next time
the taxi comes I'll be ready.

TOUCHSTONES

i. Gritstone

From his Yorkshire village he
"went up to London once—
argh, people, people, people."
He says of his wife's arrangements
of loosestrife, harebell, willow herb, foxglove,
"The trouble she takes with weeds."
With his fowling piece in '40
he "scared off" Hitler's legions.
If the moon should crumble he'd yawn.

ii. Buffalo Gal

She grieves over fallen sparrows,
gives them proper burial.
Subsisting on minimum wage,
she's bought a buffalo sight unseen,
had him freighted to Texas from Montana,
boards him on a free-range ranch.
Won't wear leather shoes. Nourishes
herself on leaves, stalks, roots,
no fruit—"an ovary with seeds,
that would be eating babies."

iii. Raison d'être

Five feet three and a hundred pounds
of passion, this one feeds on venom
as saints live on the Host.
To prepare a table before him

in the presence of two from among
his scores of enemies,
then hand him a forty-five
loaded with a single bullet
would drive him to turn the pistol
on himself. One night as he
lay dying, I called him back
to life by whispering in
his ear the names of those
his death would leave unhated.

iv. Envoi

Tested against these proof rocks
the run of us crack and crumble.

MAN IN A CAGE

> "the iron cage of despair"
> —Bunyan, *The Pilgrim's Progress*

Hour after hour he sits
chin in hands. Through bars
of fingers he watches antics
of a world he has renounced.
In his eyes we read NO VISITORS.

Our nod is a ploy; our smile,
a trap; our words, a gambit.
Zipped lips proclaim his contempt
for our transparency.

Did love betray him? his daughters
throw him out of the very house
he gave them? his father fall beneath
his whip where three roads meet?
Hatched from an egg of despair,
was he nursed on adder's milk?

For him we fear tall buildings,
rigs barreling beneath bridges,
deep water, knotted ropes,
the kiss of a blue steel mouth.

He confronts his mortal enemy
when he shaves, blade in hand.

"MY FATHER MOVED THROUGH DOOMS OF LOVE"

—e e cummings

It's Sunday, the most melancholy day
of the week. Long gone to dust, my father is back
in the pulpit and my mind is going astray,

like the hundredth lamb. Sunday always seems gray
not sunny, and morning worship can exact
no reverence from me. I cannot pray.

Reluctant to leave, I knew I couldn't stay.
Hearing my father's words, I'd missed the fact:
the love he lived had made him choose his way.

I took a different tack. Offshore we lay,
bombarding Okinawa. The sky was black
with death. On that murderous Easter Day

no one was resurrected. Not boys at play,
to sink our ship they willingly took our flack—
a strange communion, since both were made of clay.

Victory's agony has made me pay
the price of following a bloody track,
believing it would lead to peace some day.
My father's love has proved the better way.

HOREHOUND AND FOX FUR

WORSHIP THE LORD IN THE BEAUTY OF HOLINESS
is arched in Gothic gold above the altar.
In the pulpit my father not my father is preaching.
The heads of crows are nodding in the choir loft.
Beneath the pew my legs in corduroy knickers
dangle, swishing as I swing them. My mother unwraps
her fox fur, lays it on my lap with a "shhh."

I touch the spongy nose, as black as sin.
Brown eyes stare, lifeless as the marbles in my pocket.
I pet his russet coat, then jerk his snout
around in search of prey, resurrecting him.

Keeping her eyes on her son in his swallow-tailed coat,
my grandmother roots in her handbag, then digs out
a lumpy hunk and presses it into my palm.

"There now, dear heart," she whispers, lips tickling my ear,
"something to suck on." Tasting the bitter mint,
I want to spit it out. Tears well in my eyes.

Softly the organ plays, "Break Thou the Bread
of Life." My two-personed father, head down, descends
to the Lord's table and removes the tented cloth
from a miniature castle of silver. To deacons, assembled
like the twelve disciples, he delivers trays,
first bearing cubes of bread, then thimbles of grape juice
to appease the hunger and slake the thirst of believers.

"Take, eat, this is my body..." My mother and
grandmother slip a bread cube between their lips.

"Likewise also the cup after supper…" They pour
a thimbleful of grape juice down their throats.

I wonder, might a morsel of flesh and sip
of blood of the man who told his friends to eat
and drink him sweeten my grandmother's horehound?

Years later I'll read it was widely believed the Devil
could change himself into the shape of a fox.

BEYOND WORDS

When the smile you tendered me that evening
as I left flashed in memory
the instant mother whispered on the phone,
"Your father's gone," I knew you had known then.

How right of you to keep your secret from me.
Between us we both mistrusted words.

Watching the god for whom you spurned
the world you'd courted young, whose hand
you might have won, torment you like a devil
while you embraced him, angered me to anguish.

Night after night, confined in consciousness
by that unbribable turnkey, brain,
I dredge up from the dark what I never dared
to tell you. The rest is silence.

DAY BY DAY

skull is effacing face,
bones become brittle as icicles,
muscles ignore commands.

After years of darkening,
his eyes still turn toward light.
He's floating out of time.

With nary a fond good-bye,
he's leaving this too too solid world
to drift through cloudscapes where
architecture shifts shape, sculpture
is protean, colors bleed.

From a home that's not his home,
where words are broken silence and
thought is more fugitive than smoke,
the shreds of his dignity will
be hauled off to the dumpster.

As streams of our grief run dry,
we draw from deep wells of wonder.

PASSAGE OF A PAINTER

i. Missing Him

I've come to visit in Assisted Living.
Beyond assistance, he isn't here.

Concealed in the false ceiling
above the bed I stop beside,
a marionette master is jerking
unseeable strings hooked on hands and feet.

When I take one hand to bestow the peace
of rest, it wants my hand to dance.

I whisper his name, then mine
into a porcelain ear.

It's pointless to whisk away the fly,
persistent as a spy plane
that's on to something,
buzzing eyes that never blink.

To excuse myself for living,
I kiss a marbled forehead,
then steal away.

ii. Finding Him

On a country lane I try
to walk it off, telling myself,
look, look, look.

The colors of his palette
rival the blue of chicory.

In the intricate geometry
of Queen Anne's lace, find
sanction for his composition.

Prolific as black-eyed Susan,
he's modest as daisy fleabane.

The timely fading and drooping
of the blossoms of day lilies
mimic his acquiescence.

Renouncing words as he
abandons flesh, he's snug
in the trumpet of morning glory,
twisting among corn stalks,
feed for the coming winter.

His soul, if such mystery
can be manifest,
inhabits the butterfly,
a monarch who, wings folded
like praying hands, sucks
ambrosia from red clover.

REQUIEM FOR A COMPOSER

John Davison, 1930-1999

After a year of self-deception,
pretending zero needn't come
before there's one,
nothing before something,
this day we do begin the new millennium.

The second such mark our minds have notched
on the sand rope we call time
since Caesar Augustus decreed
a tax on being alive.
The twentieth or so since a stone's point
scratched lines on a rock face
and made then now, brought there here.
How many thousands since paws pushed bodies
upright, denying earth's claim
and introducing pain to the spine?
Before before, the row of zeroes
to the infinite, which somewhere, or nowhere,
collides with after,
stretches beyond our suppose.

Outside the window snow,
not fresh enough for a child to eat
nor firm enough carve your lover's name in
for birds or gods to see,
covers the world like newsprint.
A backward look at a century of killing
chills me to the bone. No matter what
the number we put on the moment,
our hour's close to zero.

I've found a comfort zone
between the radiator, whose heat
is hell on the sounding board,
and the bend of the grand piano.

Providing my pen a surface, the lid
on the harp is closed, like the wing
of a crow I passed on my morning walk,
shrouding its ice-black body.

So close to the tip my nose would be pollinated
should I swing my head that way,
Easter lilies, an anachronous Christmas gift,
pour out their dying fragrance,
wilting trumpets proclaim no resurrection.

Measured against what's been
and what's to come, the life
of words inside my mind is brief
as the instant snow's white's pure,
or lilies perfume their sweetest. Corruption
sets in as I commence transcribing.

Avoiding sticky gold anthers,
I turn toward the music stand.
My eyes light on the score
of a nocturne and chaconne
my confrere-friend composed
while he was dying. Beyond
my fingers' skill to bring them
back to life, night song and dance
lie buried in lines and spaces.

One year before the *faux* millennium,
the ear that heard the music
inside silence closed, the hand
that noted it in black on white
went stiff as the cold crow's claw.
This day there'll be no more writing.

January 1, 2001

Soo-Min Kim Plays a Violin Sonata

Insinuating himself
between your chin and shoulder,
a dragon is going at your throat.
One hand is trying to fend
him off with a puny stick
while fingers of the other
claw at the strings of his neck.

No, no, no—
it must be you've tamed him.
In your silky pink-flowered dress
you're carrying your pet
to a teahouse. So soft his purr
it scarcely intrudes on silence.

Oh my! the ingrate has turned on you.
Might his teeth have pierced your skin?
Is he sucking your blood? Your slender arms
are struggling to hold him off
while the lashing of your ponytail
denotes your mighty will.
Shreds dangle from the whip you lash
him with. From the fierceness of your doing
your fingers must be bleeding.

The sweep of the closing cadenzas,
your triumph, takes my breath.

FAR AWAY THE TRAIN-BIRDS CRY

Two lovers I knew then
dreamed up this title for a play
that flopped in the bottomless pit
between page and stage.
I never laid eyes on the script.

The lovers have gone separate ways.
Still I see and hear those stillborn birds—
heads jeweled like pheasants',
the beady eyes of hawks,
necks serpentine as swans',
great wings that flap but seldom as they soar.

"Train" birds? Because in a time long gone
they'd follow platform cars
and snatch midair flung hunks
of bread? Were they able to hear
in the swish of wheels on steel
a promise too hush for our ears?

Might their cries have been love notes
mate to mate? laments for lovers lost?
for fledglings snakes had gobbled?

Bewitched by the whistle's wail
did they search for rest in a faraway nest,
where parallels meet? Could they
have been singing their own requiem?

Like the bird of gold that isn't,
whose song keeps a drowsy emperor,
who never was, awake,

train birds have flown and sung
for me since I first heard their name.
I've snared them for this poem.

A LA RECHERCHE DU TEMPS PERDU

I wonder what her beauty looks like now,
as I recall those hours gone, misspent
with her I ached to love, not knowing how.

Could I roll back the years, would she allow
me entrance to explore, dwell in her then
pure being? Jealously wondering by now

how many she's granted such favor to, I bow
my head and purse my lips, a penitent
rehearsing a sin I've not committed. How

passionately I wish I might endow
the two of us again with innocence.
Ruing the chances we wasted, here and now

I'd resurrect her faultless flesh and vow
our consummation would be a sacrament,
could we kiss off the past and make then now.
To repossess time lost I don't know how.

EROS AND THANATOS

Afterward, when I've lost you to sleep,
your back toward hell, your face
toward heaven, she comes, whispering sweet
nothings in my ear—the embrace

of emptiness, the peace
of silence, the beauty of dark,
the ease of release
from being. Faint of heart,

I'm saved by the dying of night,
when you roll toward me, touch,
and, roused by the advent of light,
wrest me free from her clutch.

As she goes, the impudent slut
hisses, "My time's up but
you can bet your life I'll be back,
bringing my aphrodisiac."

DAZZLING

It's over. As hearts stop thumping
and programmed digits move,
blinking and jumping
ahead on clock's face, love's

flame that wooed
us, mating moths, cools. The hole in time
our fire burned stands proof
we'd left the clockwork world behind.

In passion's afterglow mind-sight
reviews the wasted past
and glimpses ahead of morning light
the unknown that's to come. Bed-blaze can't last.

Still, neither bygone fizzle nor coming frazzle
can undo our timeless dazzle.

FROM *RANDOM NECESSITIES*
1999

BLUE MUSHROOMS

For Katherine

Had you been there too
early this evening, and were it true
as was thought before Newton prismed,
that we see because eyes hurl
rays infused with color
into the stuff of the world,
it couldn't have come out of you,
not even from your eyes, such blue.

Nor did those mushrooms I stumbled on assume
their hue from the light of the moon
who was not in the phase
we attribute to her in the phrase
once in a..., and who
was not in the mood we adjure
her by in love songs, or used to
before one of us planted his foot,
shod in an outlandish boot,
along with the Red, White and Blue
in the dust of the sea,
grotesquely invoking Pacific, we
misnamed Tranquility.

I swear I'll never look
in the useful sort of book
that warns you to beware
of this or that because if you
feast on it, it will melt, thaw, resolve
your flesh into a dew.

Nor will I ever involve
myself in taxonomy to learn if there,
rare and till now unsung, is
a Basidiomycetes fungus
colored Madonna blue.

If only somehow we knew
which part of Himself God, Who's said
to number the hairs of our head
(and pubes?), to mark each sparrow's fall
(and droppings?), expresses in the blue
of this elfin parasol,
then perhaps we'd understand
something of the plan,
intent and purpose of it all.

To hell with science and theology.
Now after my discovery
of a once in a lifetime class of mushroom,
night is around us close as a room,
sward's soft as a mattress, air's warm
as a comforter. Come,
led me lead you to
this grove of tiny blue
trees. Not on, for goodness' sake,
but beside them we can make
an alfresco bed. Like a pair of doves
nesting, we'll bill and coo,
but just for a while, love,
until we do.

ALFRESCO

i
Past laurel, rhododendron,
white dogwood,
false Solomon's seal
and foamflower under trees.

That giant hemlock,
uprooted,
must feed on air.

More graceful than any limbs
a blacksnake slithers
into a crevice.

Mere flutter of a seraph's wing
would rend the veil
of stillness.

Only the purl of water,
mew of a dove.
"A wilderness of sweets."

ii
Betimes the bed
betides us.
Moss for a mattress,
spongy log for a pillow.
Fern is our covert.

Snake charmer
how you handle me!

The serpent within me
knows the moment.

As aeons collapse
to an instant
a reptile sprouts wings.

Beneath us lie
the possibilities
of eagles.

LOVE AND WAR

For Karl Shapiro

On our hands, blood—
blood from our buddies
innocent blood, blood of the beaten.
In our eye, flashes from hits
on water and land, in the sky.
In our ear, the concussive blast
of our own main batteries, and yes,
shrieks and moans and whimpers
afterward in nightmares.
Was it the stink of our own salty bodies
or the stench of flesh we'd never seen
but knew had roasted in the ovens
we'd turned their cities into?

Homeward bound, moored in Pearl Harbor,
we went sprinting from the landing craft
to open arms, and legs.
By the time we had undone
our thirteen buttons in the shack
of her we'd picked, we'd gone
erect as the barrels of ack-ack guns
scanning the skies for "Bettys"...
the one with two gold teeth
and a rose tattooed on her thigh;
the curry-breathed, pear-hipped one
with moss on her belly;
the still half-child who twittered,
"Say-lo, say-lo am I good for you?"
while her dainty little feet
fluttered about my head like butterflies.

How many years it's taken
to realize those oceanic girls
who, like salt water, lapped
and laved and solaced us,
the wounded ones, were peris,
heavenly beings imprisoned
in human flesh! Not to reward
us for forced continence
while we obediently killed.
Nor to take the edge from us
before we bedded the bodies
we'd defended, waiting at home
for our return in triumph.
No, no—they put us to love's test:
would we touch them gently?
use them kindly? be grateful
for their favor? give beyond
the pittance they dared ask?
—those fallen angels who
tendered us their being?

BASTARDS

Our mother told us stories about a father
we've never seen, who lives far off—his wealth
and power, his care for us, his love. Now grown,
we find it hard to swallow our mother's line.

Knocking about in the world on our own, we've learned
the rights and wrongs, the do's and don't's she taught
us at her knee are fool's gold, will-o'-the-wisps.
The axis our earth turns on is not "what should."

And what did he provide for us, this father?
Estates, yes. But failing to designate whose is which
and where, he set us at each other's throats,
destroying what he gave us by fighting over it.

Regularly our mother gathers us together
in the house our father built, a stony place,
grander than need be. Dilapidated now,
it would take a pretty penny to renovate.

We're all for tearing it down. In widow's weeds,
while claiming her spouse still lives, our mother nags:
"Make peace, my children for your father's sake—
trust, forbear, forgive, show kindness, love."

Love…the word sticks in my craw. Love vicious brothers?
scheming sisters, a putative father? a mother who,
forked-tongued, threatens us with her authority
and encumbers our rightful inheritance?

Not only have we doubts this man's our father,
we wonder about this woman. Is she our mother?
Isn't not knowing whether or not we're orphans
reason enough to act like a bunch of bastards?

CHRISTMAS EVE

Mother's hips, my first crib,
have broken. They're held by pins.
Her feet are wheels.
In her quicksand brain
I'm a sinking memory.

As I kiss her good-bye, I eye
a twelve-inch Christmas tree
on her bedside table.
Tinseled plastic, it accords
with the decor of her nursing home.
I could water it with tears.

Grief consumes high octane.
The needle's close to empty.
Thank God for Exxon and a roadhouse.

On the television screen
above the bar, a pop tart
in hot pants and a halter,
crimsoned and trimmed like Santa's suit,
go-go's. In deference to the Christ Child,
about to be born for the nineteen hundred
and ninety-sixth time, the rock and roll
she's writhing to is muted
in favor of a carol, lauding virginity,
that blares from the stereo.
Eye's out of sync with ear.

At the bar, boomerang-shaped,
singles are making moves
with the predictability of rut.

The cups of the barmaid runneth
over with breasts—a gift
from on high or silicone?

It's the darkest deep of the year.
While Muzak now blares "Joy
to the World" I sip a dry martini.
Lust and grief won't mix.

As I head for home, my sky
mark's not a star above a barn.
It's the horny moon
cradling a bundle of darkness.

MY FATHER'S TIME AND MINE

Moving across the face that bends
the linear infinite to an earthly round,
so we can bear it, hands shaped
like arrows measured my father's ministrations.

Every morning his forefinger and thumb
would spin the little wheel on a stem
to keep his time from exhausting.

No winding can restart
his run-down heart.
He's boundless now.

Jumping from one bar that marks the minutes
to the next, the second hand
describes how I snatch at pleasure.

When my mother handed down
my father's watch, I replaced
the fob, a cross of gold,
with a love knot of base metal.

ON BECOMING ORPHANED

Before, you paid no mind to knowing
you were in her mind. Always.
When her thought was on something else.
When she was sleeping. Even when,
sunk in the quagmire her softening brain
had turned to, you were unthinkable,
still you lived on in her,
nourished, cherished, homed.

Like her, you swaddled your begotten
in your mind. Held them ever after,
though more and more they weren't
the instant's thought. Reserved some room
for them after you'd seen them go,
knowing to have a mind of their own
they had to rid that place of you,
as you had done to her.

And yet, and yet,
at that great divide between
having and not having
a mother-mind to dwell in,
you felt a tremor in your core
as the last breath of her
sucked hard to take you with it.

YOUNG WIDOW

Frost on the blade of the moon,
frost on the claw of the owl,
frost on the scale of the sycamore,
frost on the nose of the mouse.

Frost in the laugh of the loon,
frost in the chained hound's howl,
frost where the wind makes the lake lap shore,
frost in the creak of the house.

In the year's first icy dawn
yesterday's widow wakes.
She hears but can't believe her brain:
'you must get up and start.'

Frost on the brown of the lawn,
frost on the cedar shakes,
frost inside the windowpane,
frost in the cleft of the heart.

HANNAH

My darling palindrome,
silence is your dwelling place.
The words you see and draw in air
are no more quick to die,
come closer to what they signify
than those we voice and hear.

Not one whit less
than the fingers that speak
for you and the eyes you read
the world with,
I love your immaculate lips,
your virgin throat, and—
dare I say it?—those ornaments of flesh,
your perfectly sculpted ears.

Dear child of my dear child,
whenever I'm driven wild
with sorrow knowing you
will never hear the music
the love that contrives this poem
is striving for, I tell
myself your inside ear
is tuned to those far sweeter, far
far sweeter melodies of silence.

Would the Emperor of Breath
and Breathlessness deny him entrance
to the heavenly Spheres of Music
had Beethoven been born deaf?

HOOKED RAM

Nosing us they bolt to a cul-de-sac,
where, come fall, they'll flock together for
the annual slaughter. At our approach they hurl
themselves against a dry-stone wall.

The ram leaps high enough to hook
a horn in the wire strung on top.
Rampant, neck twisted, he hangs,
left hoof pawing air, right flailing stones.
Ewes and lambs scoot back to open pasture.

Paralyzed by ram's frenzy, I foresee:
wool blood-soaked from stone chafe,
leg bone jutting through skin,
eyes bulging as the sinews
of his neck garrote him,
struggle dying into consummate exhaustion.

Without hesitation she flings herself
atop him, arms down his flanks, hands
grasping legs to stop their thrashing,
thighs vising haunches—as if she were a ewe
delivering a sheep upside down.

"Don't just stand there, unhook him!"
Taking his head in my hands, I feel
wool oil and stone skull, smell lanolin.

Ram terror deadlocks man strength.
To lever his head, I grab
the unhooked horn, using his skull
as a fulcrum. Dumbly he submits.

As horn tip clears the wire,
my hand's flung off. It snags
on a rusty barb. Heaving her off
backward, the ram runs free.

Wondering when last I was shot
with tetanus antigen, I pinch
and squeeze the puncture.
It refuses to bleed. I suck, then spit.
My spittle comes out white.

At the dead-end wall we climb
a stile. Hard as I draw, bad blood
won't run. I can't get out
a word. My jaw feels locked.

SIGN IN THE LONDON UNDERGROUND

To keep this terminal rendezvous
you have to travel underground.
"All trains go to Waterloo."

You leave the glittering avenue
with many a pang, for you are bound
to keep a darker rendezvous.

You pay your pound and pence, pass through
the turnstile, drop three levels down
to tracks that lead to Waterloo.

The car is empty save for you.
Electric it skates beneath the town
and river toward your rendezvous.

Driven by an unseen crew,
shrieking like a stricken hound,
the train brakes into Waterloo.

When you gave in to dark you knew
how bare and silently profound
you'd find your platform rendezvous.
"All trains go to Waterloo."

ORGAN PRELUDE

Head bowed above the manuals,
she's summoning the will
to raise her hands and plunge
fingers on the keys, to stab
the wooden pedals with her toes.

We're held within the silence
that presides
before anything begins
and reigns
when everything is finished.

During this parenthesis
sperm snakes toward an egg,
a brain cell can't remember,
a heart gives up beating.

Earth's middle, where the poles conjoin,
is dark to our instruments
as the backside of a moon
circling a planet looping
a star we haven't surmised.
What in God's name does or doesn't
between those swirls of light?
And the whole black negative empty other.

We're falling, falling, falling
into the maw of chaos when
the opening chord comes crashing
through time's hairline.

Then Bach's *Die Kunst der Fuge*
reorders space and time for us
for forty minutes.

THE CARYATID

In memory of Mildred Martin

No wind could sway her—impervious
to rain and flung debris,
to summer's melt and winter's chill.

The earth's disseverance by a moon
amok or an atom teased beyond
endurance wouldn't have fazed her,
matriarch of understatement.

Even then, say all had come apart,
she'd have raised an eyebrow,
affirming the absurdity, and cocked
a smile, her ultimate ironies.

So much she upheld, held up so many.
Attracted to earth's lode, her feet
came to resent the lure of motion.

Unwilling to reckon in hours,
she dismissed those days, aeons ago
it seemed, when she'd caught us with
a question, pinned us to a fact,
disarmed us with an "oh...?"

remembering only the crack of a stick
of chalk, brittle as her bones would grow,
when she'd snap it to prevent the screak
while she hieroglyphed on slate...
oh, the dust from those sticks on her fingers!

Veils dropped over her eyes,
weary of a show gone stale.
As she listened less and less,
she fathomed silence more.

Finally it's the heart.
The instant she accomplished stillness,
the fist at her core was clenched
on a love hard enough to survive
the assaults of the new barbarians,
yes, the fiercest fire,
and, still more deadly,
the dilapidations of slow time.

BALLET ALEATORIC

For Rachel

Breezes are playing around
the mimosa. Getting an eyeful
down under, I see a skyful
of pink and white tutus upside down.

On a stage of blue they dance
without any bodies inside,
their every movement determined by
the choreography of chance.

ON BUSINESS FROM PORLOCK

What does it all add up to
or come down to? None of our claims
are valid yet we have to account.
Reason enough to master stealth.

Nothing we stuff in time's wound
can staunch the bleeding. We have
a weary muscle up our sleeve.

All our becauses are symptoms
without a cure. Tell children playing
ring-around-a-rosy about the pox?

It's a stare-down before a cracked mirror
and sooner or later the man
on business from Porlock arrives.

Runagate

Flown from the world of my father, I need
a bath. Dirt crescents beneath my fingernails.

At last, a tub—horse trough mounted
on four of Regina Victoria's feet—
in Lutterworth, where Wycliffe Englished
Scripture. Water smokes as it gushes.

Out the window—a gibbous yew,
a spruce haphazard against the sky,
a pine whose limbs twist to
the shape paired lovers make
in Hell's first circle of punishment.

I wade through steam and climb into the tub.
Ouch! pain is the price of cleansing.
Compelling flesh to submit itself to heat,
I kneel like a penitent, then roll onto
my back. Head angled forward by
the upslope of the porcelain, I'm a man
on the horizontal being hanged.
The hovering nimbus is a self-wraith
against whom I shut my eyes.

My mind runs on...slambang!
The afterimage of the bathroom window
of this old manse-like house is set
in the wall of the little clapboard chapel,
my father's charge, some three thousand miles
behind me. I'm six. I'm back in the pew.
It's Sunday morning. All of us gathered
together here are colonists of the Lord.

Three panels of stained glass windows
within an arch that points toward Heaven—
the Trinities of childhood are my Furies.

A heart-stitch flips me over onto my belly.
I lash like a harpooned whale. "One son,"
I sob, "can't stop the tide of history."
Scarcely will my salt tears brine the bath.

Gradually I come calm. The water turns
lukewarm as the church at Laodicea. I feel
so limp were some imp to pull the plug
I'd slither down the drain, leaving as
my last will and testament a ring of dirt.

Recreant at Winchester

Sinful with creature comforts the inn
stands in the cathedral's shadow.

A stone's throw from our window,
beneath God knows how many tons
of stone in cruciform, bed bones
of Saxon kings. The few sound teeth
this uncouth royalty might claim,
dice in dust inside their stony boxes,
amount to little.

Surrounding the sanctuary,
skulls of bishops rest face-up
in sepulchers. Their empty sockets
stare at their own backsides in effigy,
their only ken till doomsday. It's looming,
though not quite in the way they believed.

Tower bells toll the passing
of the hour. Seconds after
the cathedral's brilliant fanfare,
a parish clock clanks.
Midnight has just struck, twice.
The time is out of joint.

Apart, the pair of trundle beds our room
provides serve the chaste, jaded and unable.
Coupled, they accommodate honeymooners,
fornicators, and adulterers,
as well as married lovers. We hitch
them together. Against our thrashing
the seam holds tight. It's a steamy night.

Afterward, salt-slick as seals, we uncouple
the beds. Through the slit where the drapes don't meet
moonlight knifes. We've used up all our voices—
cherub coos, animal groans, demon sobs.
On separate slabs we lie in the almost dark,
wan effigies of spent bodies.

Tomorrow's my birthday. Dressed Sunday,
teeth brushed and flossed, we'll attend the cathedral service.
Allowing for clock time three thousand miles
to the west, where my wind-blown forebears,
deracinated weeds, re-rooted
and scattered seed, the choir will be rendering
the antiphon while I was being
spanked alive fifty-nine years ago.

The chapter dean's to preach. A pair
of graceless lovers we'll be sitting
a little apart from the faithful while,
joined as a single body, they
eat the flesh and drink the blood
of the god they love and devour.

Sleep, a teasing imp, dances beyond
my fingertips. Snatching at it, I teeter,
almost fall into the fissure between our beds.
Denied the peace that passes, I lie detached,
waiting for the double strike of time.

De Mowbray's Men Re-Consecrate a Church

Black Death doing his dance from town
to farm to castle. Pilfering, poaching,
trespassing, haggling, complaining. Stiff backs
and stony faces. Heathen curses. Arrows
from unseen bows. Lightning in winter.
Miasmal mist a doom upon this isle.

Year in, year out we promised, cajoled,
threatened, impressed whipped, mutilated, killed.
One December afternoon we were able to say
"*fini*": the walls now thick enough for triple doors,
as in Coutances; clerestory and lunettes
beneath the roof we'd raised to a proper height;
the square bell tower we'd added casting
scarcely a shadow across the grayness
of the day. Massively it squatted,
God's stronghold upon earth.

Silent inside after the sound
of our sollerets had rung throughout the nave
and, caroming off the peers, had resounded
down the bays—thunder rattling away
across the hills. All expectancy.

Defying our upturned eyes and hearkening ears
the magus or priest we dragged from St. Oswine's
refused to proceed, muttering we knew why.
He stank in his rags. De Laigle tried suasion
in Saxon, then decreed in the Conqueror's tongue.

Clam-lipped, turbot-eyed, hands clapped
against thighs to make himself seem armless,
the rascal bawled to some pagan god

for brazen courage. Only after right there
in the rectified sanctuary my mailed fist
called forth some blood from his face,
would he sign the Cross, chant formulary words,
invoking a damnable ghost for all we could tell.
His voice sounded hollow as an echo.

At the wonted time we clanked to our knees on
the slates, ruffled beards against our gorgets. Our
responses hung heavy as smoke from damp turnips.

As enfilade we jangled out the western portal,
some swine of a lunatic, mucked up
to his shanks, began to revile us, mocking
our handiwork, summoning drought, flood,
famine, pestilence, fire, and sword, charging
Hell's jaws to open and snatch us.

A volley of leftover stones felled him.
When de Laigle, removing his gauntlet,
crammed a hand in the mouth of the maniac,
grabbed his tongue, spotted like a fish, between
forefinger and thumb, and stretched it full-length,
I neatly sliced off inches with my falchion.
The bloody orphan was snatched by a starveling cur
that seemed to belong to the madman.

The Presence we believe will come in time.

VILLAGE CHURCH, YORKSHIRE

On the Cross draw a line from the top
to the arm ends: that's the roof pitch.
A timeless tower squats on the nave,
head on a hunchbacked dwarf.

Lay the Cross on the ground. Around it
wall a rectangle: that's roughly the size of it.

Now use some poetic license and imagine
they were building it just as He was being nailed.
The bell rope might tickle his toes. They'd leave
gaps in the walls for low portals, so to enter
at His knees. Off the aisle of His spine,
His ribs for standing (pews won't come
for centuries) during the service.
The hollow at the bottom of His throat
would serve as a baptismal font.
In the sacred wounded head the sanctuary
would be sited: the low communion rail,
His mouth; His eyes the pulpit and lectern;
the silk reredos, His hair. Oh, how
they prayed He would enter into these stones!

They had such fearful doubts, those builders:
surviving winter, hunger, the Black Death,
axes, swords and firebrands wielded by giants
with flame-red beards and flowing manes,
gaining access to water the beaver-like monks
at Rievaulx were diverting eastward from them;

that inside the gauntleted fist of de Mowbray's
Norman henchman some gentilesse lay;

that after the spiking and hoisting He
really had come back; that He could and would
stand by them here and hereafter—

so hard to make out of the Roman letters what
had happened so long ago in a far-off place.
No wonder they named these stones they piled St. Thomas.

This village, whose heart mistrusted, stands
cursed, an untimely fig tree. What
few progeny there are go crooked
as the lanes and cottages theirs fathers made.
While others in this fertile valley
prospered, this miscreant talent hid
itself in earth, against their Lord's return.

Behind padlocked grates, oak of both doors
is split in lightning jags. Beneath mesh wire
protecting six windows like a hauberk,
opaque glass depicts nothing. A notice tacked
to a signboard announces services in
St. Michael's, Coxwold; St. Cuthbert's, Crayke;
St. Anthony's, Scawton, every third Sunday.
Even their doubt gave out.

A tare in a croft of wheat,
I belong here.

MAKING OUT THE STONES

At Tintern Abbey

Staring across the Wye, I see
stones in a graveyard shuffle.
I blink—the stones turn into sheep,
the graveyard becomes a meadow.

In a pasture beside, a pair of bays
and a skewbald pony are grazing.
The horses' legs have been bred so thin
as to take the breath. Their necks are writhing,
trying to throw off their heads. No wind
to excite them this afternoon. It must be flies.
In the quiet I hear a whinny that sounds
demonic. The pony champs stolidly.

In the high field above the pasture
ingots of baled wheat shine. No tractor
has the instinct for all fours needed to work
that slope. It calls for Clydesdales or Shires.

On the bank near where I'm sitting, stones
of the abbey ruin flash with falling sunlight.
Unroofed walls and buttresses supporting
nothing throw gigantic shadows,
silhouettes of sauropods that perished
in the great Cretaceous debacle.

Beside the sluice a stone mill crumbles.
A scattering of implements in the race
is rusting to ore. Among some rushes
half a grindstone is visible.

The tower of the parish church barely transcends
treetops on the hill above the ruin.
Over this village in hiding hangs a cloud—
England with Scotland chopped off
at the neck, Wales from the butt.
The cloud's an impure white. Hearing
the drone of an engine, I eye-rove
the sky until I spot a cross,
black against gray. It's heading east.

Brown-capped, drab-winged, speckled
on back and tail, gulls ride the tidal Wye.
Chepstow's their port of entry.
Canny birds—fewer beaks,
more bread here, seven miles upstream.

The water looks viscous enough to bear
the jilted Ophelia, with help from her swelling belly
and spreading skirts. No Dane, she's pure English.
Resquiescat in pace, the current murmurs
as she chants her bawdy lays. When milfoil
tentacles entangle her, under she goes.
The stream will serve as her winding sheet.

Moored to a drum, a boat floats motionlessly.
The white of its hull and blue of its cabin
declare its attachment to the white house,
trimmed with blue, stuck in the hillside above.
In the horseshoe drive stands a pick-up,
fire-engine red. The pastoral ends here.

A gull takes off. Timed like planes jetting
from a carrier's flight deck, the covey follow.
Heading downstream, they wheel toward

the Channel. The cross-shaped plane's disappeared.
Hearing a marching song, I visualize
rucksacks and lederhosen before I see
a phalanx of rock-hard legs come stomping
across the bridge nearby. A banner proclaims:
THIS OUTING CLUB HAS FOOTWALKED FROM BAVARIA.
Did the Channel waters divide or bear
them up? To cross that ditch in '40
was not so easy. His *Spazierstock*
at the ready, their leader would take on
Robin Hood—just for the sport. Dresden
and Coventry have been rebuilt.
It's the 80s and all is forgiven.

As I stare, my eye reconstructs the abbey.
Toward it, up the cart road a team of oxen
drags a cannon, snub-nosed as the King.
Heretic Henry, still smarting from the fall
Francis of Valois administered in the Field
of the Cloth of Gold, and tired
of committing incest on Aragon silk,
is urgent for adultery on English linen.
His right hand, raw-beef red with the blood
of Thomas More, rams home the charge.
His left, dripping the sizzle of poor John Frith,
applies the flaming linstock.
Devastating walls that have borne
the Cross for centuries, that shot
resounds in France, Castile and Rome.

Henry Tudor looked ahead.
While the thundering of his engines
deadened the royal ear to the wail
of peers on the wheel, the squeal
of bishops in the boot, his lust

for Spanish and English meat
carved out the shape of history.

How can we impeach him, we who
traject his cannon into the sky?
A cross without arms, pointed east,
it's poised to bring premiers,
prime ministers and presidents,
popes, cardinals and priests,
to say nothing of the sheep,
trembling to their knees.

INFIDEL IN ROME

In the *cappella* of the *Palazzo Barberini*
I can almost pray.
It's thirteen lengths of my shoe
by seventeen, was frescoed in the day
of high baroque by *il pittore Romanelli*
and his crew.

Look down at the tiled floor.
Imagine you're gaping at the door
that keeps the lid on chaos. There see a sun
exploding—an aeon's fun
caused and enjoyed in one
instant of destroy/restore.

Your skeptical eye acknowledges tromp l'oeil
only when your fingers move
around a fluted column and find it smooth.
Leftover from late Rome,
four clones of Venus' naked boy,
passed off as cherubs, hang inside the dome,

attendant on the Paraclete,
who, embodied in a dove,
hovers on wings unmoving between their beat.
The cycle has no start or end
so your eye must follow the chapel's ovoid bend
from the first flutter in the womb of Love

to its final elevation,
then back to reincarnation
and round again. Between, a life: his birth
in a mandated place in a hostile time; trying

carpentry, teaching, doctoring; failing;
dying young, a criminal; burial in a stranger's earth.

Now stop your eye where they're resting
while on the run
to Egypt. It's not the smile
of the father as he extends
a fleshy apple. Nor the glee of the son
who's being lured into the step that ends

the mother's hold
on him. Nor the parted in consternation lips
of her, whose hands still mold
just-gone fat little hips
in the air.
It's the stare

on the face
of the donkey peeping around a tree,
in whose bestial knowing you can see
prescience of its rueful place
in the palmy parade that five days later will
halt on the skull-shaped hill.

UNBECOMING IN ITALIA

i

We wake to the hiss of geese on the rampage—
tires squishing through water on the Via Veneto.
Our shutters open on the Aurelian Wall,
the look of slave hands still on its bricks,
the color of rotting carrots.
Arches serve as niches for artists and pigeons.
Both have an eye out for something to scavenge.
Above the coping the tops of pines
inside the Borghese Gardens rise
like giant broccoli. Were the sun to show
its face, I'd bite my thumb at it.

Yesterday, Monday, a holiday in Rome,
I cringed and whined and festered.

Easter morning in Naples we
were blocked in an intestine *via*
off the Piazza Garibaldi by a human juggernaut.

White-robed children, nuns and priests
wagged last Sunday's palms and hymned
the Resurrection while high on a pole
Christ triumphant swayed above the masses.

Did the fingers that stripped me of my proof
of being belong to released Barabbas?
to the forgiven thief boomeranged from promised
Paradise to this dirty recidivous world?

After some coffee and an insipid croissant,
I present my nonexistent self

at the U.S. embassy, a showy palazzo
bequeathed to the State Department by
the general who appropriated it
for his headquarters when the Nazis
tucked their tails and ran for home.

Just inside the gate invisible fingers
frisk my anonymous body, vouch
for its fecklessness. Without credit
I grovel before the lowest of the low.

For ten thousand lira, borrowed, I procure
from a nearby photo shop the likeness of
a spy, exposed, condemned, trying for
a second lease on life by ratting on himself.
I'll be anyone they say I am.

ii
The night of the theft and the night after,
bruised and benumbed, I held myself aloof.
Last night, still mortified, though born again,
I kneaded her flesh four times—first frantic,
then wild, then fierce, then desperate.

Over another morning coffee and croissant,
our secular communion, my eyes avoid
her out of shame. I can't escape
a savage urge to prowl Rome's streets and rape.

THE SECOND-BEST HOTEL IN CHAMBERY

How many lifts were left, we had to wonder,
hearing the groan of the cables, as the car
shuddered while stuttering us up.

Pock-marked, painted and repainted
like the cheek of a demimondaine,
the bed hogged most of the room.
On the dresser one wooden knob
was intact. One was missing.
The rest were broken, moons
in various phases. A sky going dark,
the mirror was a shower of stars.

From the ceiling, a sepia map
of unknown seas and continents,
a bald light bulb dangled on a neck
of cord knotted on itself. The frame
of the window was a coffin standing on end.

In the cobbled courtyard four floors down
a refrigerator, ancien régime, crowned
with its own works, reigned over
garbage cans, cartons of trash,
scattered sheets of newsprint.

Though we paid the one-night price, the room
would give us nothing of itself.
We couldn't help thinking heart failure,
bloody sheets, rope around the throat.
No Joseph would lead his Mary to that bed.

Lumpy as the foothills toward Chamonix,
the mattress kept our bodies
from doing their level best.
A squeaking bedspring served
as the singing master of our souls.

ON THE CORNISH COAST

At Tintagel ocean's been licking
a cave in the cliff, been spending itself
in the cove since before you were undine,
I water snake. Rock acquiesces.
In the long run time can tame what's violent,
love sometimes works its way
on earth, shaping sheer beauty.

In the room overlooking this scarp,
while your feet paddled air in abandon,
my eyes flashed back through eons
of division, watched toes emerge
from a web, watched ankles, knees
and thighs divide like twins,

saw all the way back to the cleft,
the primal wound healed,
flesh pain turned to joy,
coral-lipped, conch-pink, nacre-slick.

My eyes gave out in your whorl,
you took me back to the eel.

Louder than salt sea moan
a bell buoy rang,
calling a warning,
a summons from the now.

Undertow proved stronger,
sucked us limp as seaweed
into the cavern of sleep.

These are afterwords.
You understand. During
there are no correspondences,
only doing.

THE CUTTING

Swallows swoop over, loop
under the bridge,
cutting figure eights
in the thickening air.

For the humming bird never to emerge
from the tangle of honeysuckle
we watched him dart into
is a frightening suppose.

In the sluice below, water
idling from the lake toward the chasm,
is powerless to free the branch hung up
on the dam. When a rain spate sends it over,
we won't be perched on this railing.

Wind blew the seeds we've sprung from
to their rooting sites. Besides
the mischance of places, our timing is off.
I've gone rotten from waiting.

I gape at that huge orange gouge in earth's side
deep in the gorge. Beyond
where water smashes itself on the rocks,
the pool's dark blood.

Never believe denial's the father
of good. Desire's ravisher,
it begets that bastard pain.

I cringe before shadows of children
who never will be. I make love
to you with a scalpel.
Love itself is a sparrow's flight
through a great hall where
fire blazes on a winter night,
a parenthesis in the dark.

Now trees on the shore transform
themselves to silhouettes.
Trees mirrored in the lake
dissolve into black water.

Though the beaver hasn't revealed himself,
teeth marks in felled pines
are proof his genius presides.

OYSTERS

i
Barnacle-covered, the color and weight
of zinc, dredged from the sand
and shingles of some Carolina inlet,
life locked in a rock.

The oyster knife won't split them.
I, determined housebreaker, jimmy
and pry them open with a chisel.

We've arrived at this point
between ocean and sound
during storm, hungry and late,
with a bottle of gin and the oysters.

ii
Slick-fingered abortionists, we
scrape their flesh from its mother-of-pearl,
swallow them raw. Mucous,
they slither down our throats, martyrs
making smooth their own rough ends.

Cannibal as sharks we pinch and gulp
the tiny crabs that scurry in the shells.
Our teeth grind grit, we spit potential pearls,
then flush our mouths with gin.

iii
After the booze and the oysters
it's the bed. Both of our marriages
broken, our children caught
between tide and the undertow,

we writhe to make a match,
half shells that don't quite fit.

At the zero hour we trust
the little killer loop
is doing its inside job.

iv
Afterward, each clutches other,
barnacle on a barnacle.

Dozing, I move through water,
struggling against a current,
thrash to stay afloat,

while through the jalousie of sleep
I hear nor'easter's howl
whipping southward from Nantucket
and the upraised arm of Cape Cod.

BLUE DRIVE

Venus it seems I'm on or perhaps
the very bottom of the world
dipped in a blue cloud, as I drive
this pre-dawn morning through thick mist

or thin water. Straining to make out
a road sign is like trying to read smoke.
Coffee aftertastes bitter. About to loop
my machine around the southeast

petal of a cloverleaf, I flick
the direction signal. It ticks
like a time bomb. No traffic in
the mirror or ahead. Only

an automaton would give such
a pointless indication. To save
face I tell myself ghosts must
feel thus when they communicate.

Reconnoitering the concrete
my monster-mouthed Oldsmobile
is gobbling a segment at a time,
gradually I descry a whole

constellation of Betelgeuses
being born—which vision materializes
less cosmically into the rear
end of a rig. I pass three tiers
of packed-in porkers, spectators

in a rectangular colosseum
where they'll become protagonists

in unritualistic slaughter. Close
to the berm a sycamore is a tree
of mottled bone. Pines are ever-blues.
As I bridge it, the Susquehanna lies

like cooling lava. A mountain's flanks
shag like a buffalo's. It's hump
evanesces. A squashed skunk stinks.
Slowly but as surely as the hogs

go into ham, these mountains are dying
into hills. The world is ill and dying
on this obscure morning. The Gabriel voice
of Richard Tucker silenced by

Time's knife in his throat; Brezhnev stricken
with leukemia, they say; the most beautiful
girl I've ever taught roasted
to death in a cabin two nights ago.

I try to stop the intestine flow
of images by focusing on,
as in Grandmother's stereopticon,
an upcoming barn I know,

"1776" chiseled defiantly
into its limestone lintel.
To visit Father, eighty-two,
I have to navigate this blue.

SEEING MY FATHER GET THE EVENING PAPER

To know he's in that box wherein he'll be
no more, swamped with flowers,
as he beheld the crate that held what was
his mother, another what was my brother,
as he would want it strewn for us he's left,

to know he moves among those wilt-less blooms
I know bloom nowhere save where his fond belief
has seeded and nurtured them in expectation
of his transport beyond all gardens,
would be to see him on the other side of water:
shining, free, returned, secure, at peace.

To watch him drowning in his overcoat,
leant against wind,
hefting each footstep off the viscid earth,
headlong into cold,
a worn-down man trying to run, refugee
from a shell-shocked century,
blundering his way through traffic
as if the buses, trucks and cars were bombs
dropping providentially around him,
all unaware the eyes of now his only son
are looking out at him from inside one of them,

The Philadelphia Bulletin,
in which he's daily read the world throughout
a lifetime without ever having found one word
about himself, rolled tight and tucked,
a monstrous thermometer, in his right armpit,

drives me until I rage to rip
my sex off, hold it bleeding
in my hand like so much meat
for that dog Time to snatch
and tooth and eat.

DRIVE HOME

What a world of pain we drive off in!
—after a night of snow-glaze rain:
iron ice on roofs and lawns, meadows
and fields white-plated, each branch,
the utmost twig of tree and shrub and bush
vitrified, the meanest weed in glass,
crown vetch on the flanks of hills turned silver moss—
driving my life-sick father home,
only to desert him.

Through man-ground lenses his eyes
see shapeless terror. His ear, powered by
a battery, rejects the words I tender:
"It will pass, father, it always does.
You'll be at peace again." As if he were insentient,
he fails to feel the cruelty this ice imposes
on life outside. His world's reduced
to suffering within.

Above this porcelained landscape, the winter sun
glares impotently defiant as I head toward it.

He's raving about a lifelong friend, a man
he envies for calling a full week in advance
his own departure to the day—
the fiftieth anniversary of his wedding,
it turned out. His daughter had arranged
a celebration with some few leftover friends.
For seven days he'd tried to tell her and his wife.
The wedding bak'd-meats did coldly furnish forth
the funeral table. "Please call me home!
Lord, why not let me come?"

Now he's taken off his glasses, deadened
his hearing aid, wrapped his teeth
in a handkerchief and stuffed them
in his pocket. Driven by his son who
knows the way, he's marooned as any infant.

The story gives way to prayer, prayer
to a mutter, mutter to a murmur,
murmur into a snore. Every few seconds
I dart an eye at him. At first
lips flutter, then just the bottom one
trembles. At last his open mouth goes still.
Praise be! he's cut off from his lashing nerves.

Through the tinted windshield I watch
the white exhaust of an invisible jet
slowly slice the sky.

All the way it's freeze. My father sleeps
until I kill the motor in his carport.
That starts his engine, the self that grinds the self.

NULLIUS FILIUS

Death has turned my father down
how many times.
Knowing herself his one and only love,
she teases him
heartlessly as she beseeches, excites
him to hot fury
while he prays. When with her bony fingers
she plucks pure notes
of terror on the clavichord of his nerves,
he moans
a melody in counterpoint, off-key.

Near water and high places she croons her perfect pitch
in his open ear.
From in front of a moving truck, on the track
of a subway or train,
she beckons like a whore inside a doorway.
And whispers of
coal-black sleep in an earthy bed. When he
acknowledges
her call and moves her way, she coyly shakes her head
and shuts the door.
After telling him tales that bring forth tears she mocks him.

No angler ever played a fish more surely
to exhaustion
than Death has done my father—only to
unhook his lip
each time and fling him back in life before
he flops on land
his Father promised. To watch such obscene sport,
this cooch show billed

as a mystery play and not turn parricide
or stab the eyes out,
compels a son to own he's coward or bastard.

AT A CERTAIN TABLE IN A BAR

My soul is tipsy. Its props don't stand foursquare
like the trestles of doctrine that
held the souls of my forebears.
When I lean an elbow on mine, shifting my weight,

or move something, a bottle or glass, it rocks
like a card table
during an earthquake.
It wants to be shimmed, but nowhere have I been able

to find a wedge of wood or a thin flat stone
the precise thickness it needs
under a leg—which one?
I'm canny enough to know the lopsided odds

against my curing its cant by sawing off
a scantling here or there.
To surgeon without any if's
calls for a true-old-fashioned carpenter,

the kind that shored up my father's faith—so
I'll have to put up with the tilt.
What's more, when people go,
smoke vanishes, the jukebox stands dark, how jackleg built

is the haunt that houses my soul comes clear each morning.
The ceiling's unmortised
and untenoned which serves as a warning
the roof's on the verge of collapse. Not noticed

in night's whirling spectrum of color but evident
in daylight that pains the head
is the buckling bend
of window frames while over the door the templet

bellies, a threatening pregnancy of brick.
There lives no master builder
able to shore up this wreck
of a dive where my soul grows tipsier as older.

LANCELOT TONSURED WALKS THE FIELD AT DOVER

The fee-taking raven has been here.
No matter the angle between you
and the skull, the holes that once held eyes
are fixed on yours—right pit a plea,
the left an accusation. The open graves,
are they the work of hands or wind on sand?
Not all were barged by queens to Avalon.

The jaws are chapless, clench-toothed
in what could be fear or fury. And fingers
make an empty begging bowl.
The bones of their loins are naked.
Could God pull Eve, or Guinevere,
from any rib like these?

      And you, you've cast off arms
      you plied and arms that held you too,
      when this now chalky, dried-up
      fellowship was flesh and blood
      and you were the morning star.

WHAT METAPHOR EXPOSES

Your tunic, crimson, wrought with gold
lover's knots, preening parrots, and turtledoves,
draped on a tapestried chair. Bolt thrown,
making the oak door one with the granite wall.

Lying beneath a canopy, its curtains drawn,
on a silken sheet from Toulouse, you gaze
at the wrong side of holly bobs, fleurs-de-lis
and mistletoe, embroidered on fabric from Turkestan.
It's fringed with fur. Beside you a gray-eyed lady,
hair, black as raven's wing and, dancing
on her hips when she steps so prettily, now flung
across her snow-hill breasts and mead-like belly,
a last coil lost in the thicket between her thighs.
Knowing the one and thirty laws of Andreas
the Chaplain, she plays by them with art.
Together here you'll dally away the day.

Getting a jump on the sun, her baron husband
has led all able men far from the castle.
Till dark they'll harry deer, a boar or fox.

Always at your service in the box
within the adjacent chapel, a priest,
merry and indulgent, yet empowered authentically
to turn your soiled heart clean in minutes,
He keeps flesh and soul in equilibrium.

      It's all an imagined lie.
      You came to this hovel in
      a jerkin of twill,
      flung in your haste

on a broken bench. The trull
beside you on sacked straw
scarcely knows the letters of
her name. From her reeking mouth
many a tooth is missing. Numbly
her eyes stare past you.
The latch on her door
opens to all comers.

The winking oaf she lives with
took your coin for ale.
Even before it was done
you'd had your fill.

No more than fear
can titillate, can you
find hope of pardon.
The parish priest is blind
and deaf, deranged, the rumor has it.
When was the box last
entered? No one is able
to remember the thorny way
to the church, knows whether
it's survived dilapidation.

PRO CHAOS

i
Earth turns warmer,
burns itself up,
relentless exhausts itself
like the reddest star.
On it old ocean ages.
Closer to home
the proud cells sag.

ii
What does it matter? you ask,
how can it matter out there,
beyond where light whites up, reds down,
where Cronus is no devouring tyrant,
himself is subject to Chaos,
that enduring deity they only thought
they'd vanquished, those ordering demons,
who knew not what they strove for?

Here though now you are
and here you know you fade
in another fading season,
while dying to do out there,
out there beyond, past stuff
and years, where form,
commenceless and completeless
writhes at ease—no births, no deaths,
no need for resurrections.

iii
To break, break through these designations,
reduce to point the line that runs like time,
which lumps and links (the letter killeth)—
that is the struggle.

Is why our wordless songsters
and our speculators,
not earth-screwed counters of dollars
but fearless artists of the measureless,
evoke our envy, as color lords it
over line, which it abhors.
(Beyond all color, white;
beyond all white, pure dark.)

If collapsing space to graspable,
our happenings to marks
endowed us—
as with the petrified church
and the camera—
it boxed us in.

∴ the poem,
no resolution
but a struggle.

NIGHT HOWL

i
It might be sound of the whale pod,
rumbling songs of the deep
you hear while fast asleep.

Hooking you by the ear, it no sooner
drags you into consciousness
than it heaves you like a lead line
into the waking dream of what is past.

You're at sea again. December '44.
Off Cochin China swimming armadillos
prowl for merchantmen, fishing boats, sampans.
The howl is typhoon wind.

You hear water, a gargle of sea and rain
within the rush of air, feel spray,
thick as a wave, sting what's exposed
of your face, cowled in oilskin.

ii
Through the window of the dormer
you fix on a slender elm you own, it seems,
healthy to the sight but doomed you know
in its heart by a blight imported from
the nether land of Europe. You watch it yield
to wind's rape, then measure the arc
of its acquiescence against an invisible
sky outside the mullioned window,
French—Europa again.

iii
The oscillating elm trunk turns
upside down—or you do—
becomes the pendulum of a ship's clinometer,
which you, now manning headphones
on the flag bridge, watch with bugging eyes.

27 degrees starboard, 26 degrees port
28 starboard...

Hull over stacks you'll go at 30,
the sea dog of a chief has told you.
Though you are freshly salted,
you're pretty sure he's yarning—still...

iv
Lean full weight against the wind, it holds
you vertical. At first that was fun.

After hearing over TBY
that the storm wolf's breath has huffed
a seaman off the flight deck of the *Intrepid,*
then watching a destroyer—more albatross
than angel—circle his liquid grave,
even old hands, shying from more than dumps
of chamber pots, hug the inboard bulkheads,
and cling to stanchions.

In the passageway between the signal shelter
and flag plot we've slung a lifeline. Already
it's burned some skin off your palms.

With your flesh feeling heavy as a gun barrel,
you've lost all manliness.

v
Word trickles down the chain of command:
worst blow the old man's weathered
in thirty years at sea. For the old man
or the 64,000 tons of steel he captains,
you wouldn't give a rusty piss,
except to save whatever your soul may be.

Fear has shriveled your penis, shrunk
your testicles to dried prunes. Nobody jokes.

vi
Three DDs, we hear, unwitting kamikazes,
have been swamped, a thousand men in a gulp.

One, a gray ghost ship that had been riding
in the gloom, yards off our starboard bow,
you'd seen just minutes before
she'd plunged, a half-trip submarine.

Unfathomable.

The rest of us survive
to deal more death.

vii
Now you must lever yourself outside yourself,
free from your ongoing life,
even parents, wife and children,
make a stand somewhere beyond
the terror the wind had aroused.

You ought to go down,
three thousand men aboard,
into the depths of the so-called Sea of Peace.

Little more than sport or harpooning whales—
blowing junks and unarmed fishing boats
out of the water. We take no prisoners.

Oh, never-to-be-forgotten sunset,
blood on the sheet of sky, when two parachutes,
white handkerchiefs proclaiming "we surrender,"
tumble out of the "Betty" our ack-acks
turn to a crate of fire.

"Aye aye, sir, I've picked up one of them..."
in the lens of a mounted long glass,
screwing a face into focus when
a salvo of 20 and 40 mm shells
renders him shreds of himself
that still go riding softly down the sky.

Even after the unmanned chute hits water,
collapses, bobs like plankton,
our Achilles gunners, frenzied to devour raw flesh,
riddle it, mere fabric, while I shudder.

Dead ahead looms
the burning of tinder cities,
the cremation in two blinks
of a fifth of a million lives.

And after those who somehow survive,
without any guns, ships, planes, or will,
have cried "enough," our grand old man
of the sea will steam our bristling wagons
to the land of their sacred mountain,
where from darkness to false dawn we'll lob
our sixteen-inchers, 100,0000 foot-ton energy
at the muzzle, bombarding their mother soil

—for the glory of the Navy, the Academy '09.

Sire of the West, Agamemnon,
raping Eastern Troy,
destroying her ancient altars.

viii
You're back home in bed. Clock hands,
two phosphorescent fish swimming
in a wine-dark sea, tell ten of four.
How many pounds of elm falling
at such a rate from such a height
can rafters, 2 x 6ers, possibly withstand?

You see your broke-bone self
pinned upon a tree trunk
upside down.

ix
We the victors warred for
the white god, righteously.

The vanquished strung themselves
a necklace of atrocities
with which we choked them black.

x
No peace in sleep this night.
Fingerlike the elm accuses,
threatens tormentingly.
The howl increases.

You must have plunged alive
to Round One, Circle Seven, Hell.

BALLET OF THE LITTLE CROOKED LEG

> A certain lame man...at the gate of
> the temple which is called Beautiful.
>   —Acts 3:2

Somebody else's limb, her black-slacked left—
a midget's or a dog's hind leg,
the shape of Vietnam. So
hobbling on a twisted foot
in an elevated sole, she goosesteps past
the fountain, across the plaza,
in doors of glass, and through the lobby,
past elevators to
the flaring marble staircase.

Disdaining the balustrade, she labors up
how many flights? to sink,
her little crooked leg adangle,
in a cushioned seat and watch the ballet.

You sit in the mezzanine beside two lovely legs.

Chandeliers go dark, float upward,
the crimson curtain rises. And
the little crooked leg begins to grow,
bigger and bigger, becomes immense—
though still too short—casting
its shadow across the lighted stage
on which perfect fluent legs
whirl, leap and pirouette.

You lean degrees to the right,
as looking around a pillar;
the little crooked leg moves with you.

When you shunt left it follows. You swat
at it, grab for it; it passes through your hand.
You drop your jaw and snap, to eat through flesh
and gnaw the bone; you bite your tongue.
Before your eyes the little crooked leg
is jerking, spasming, thrashing in a fit.

To try to watch the ballet in your mind
you shut your eyes—
jeté, entrechat, plié in black and white,
blighted by the shadow of
the little crooked leg humping across
the stage you are imagining.

Your mind procures a butcher's saw.
High on the thigh of the little crooked leg
you point the blade. Teeth slash black cloth,
then serrate air. The little crooked leg
already has been orphaned.

You bring the mental curtain down,
flood your head with light. On the crimson drape
the shadow of the little crooked leg is performing
a pas de deux with the shadow of its twin.

When you lift your lids, all the limbs
lopsidedly dancing onstage
are little crooked legs.

WANTING TO

After extravagance, before responsibility,
we go wandering hand in hand
neither intimate nor separate—
a necessary passage between.

Geese heading north are yawping
FRAUD FRAUD FRAUD!
June has infiltrated March.

From days of rain ending yesterday
the pond has deepened enough to float
a log, with a monstrous knob of root,
we watched all winter locked in ice
like a sauropod frozen in time.
As we walk the northern crescent I miss
hitting the wooden creature with three stones,
then score with a fourth that thuds, caroms, plops,
rippling the muddy water.

Flank brushing flank we climb the steep hill
studded with two-hundred year old oaks,
all ailing or dying, young maples and poplars,
scattered hemlocks and cedars.

My free fingers keep feeling their bark
for communion. Might touch pass through me
to you, through trees to the earth?

Twigs of the saplings and scrub growth
in the old high meadow swell red.
Painful as boils they look. Where skin

has given way, we see the most tender green.
I could weep with hurt and joy.

On top we stop. There among Dutchman's-breeches,
fat as if filled with prosperous burgher's thighs,
where the big trees start again, we come on
the bloodroot you promised—above
long pink legs, white skirts pleated
around sun-gold middles. Though the leaf
overmatches the bloom, how delicate
its veins! Its edge would make
an intricate coastline on a lush green island,
ideal for smugglers and pirates. When I touch
a waxy petal, can you feel excitement rise?

Running through bracken and bramble,
I brush aside scratching.

As returning we close the circle by
looping the south end of the pond,
around me I still am carrying
the warm wet feel of you,
which aura-ed each flower and sprig.
To know you bear something of me
from blossom to blossom, bee-like,
creates a contentment.

Afterward, noting the snake-shaped welts
on my forearms, red rivers charted on a map,
as if my veins ran open,
I realize I caught on those spikes,
wanting to.

MAUD GONNE TO WILLIAM YEATS

> Marriage is more than four bare legs in bed.
> —Medieval maxim

No banns from Rome; let's be true loves instead.
I'll be your Maud forever; you my Will.
Marriage is more than four bare legs in bed.

They knotted off blood from many an Irish head.
Apart, we're hanged; together we can kill.
No marriage knot; let's be true loves instead.

To consummate our love you have me bled
upon a stage—show Eire as a skull-shaped hill.
Marriage is more than four bare legs in bed.

In this, our ancient holy land the dead
still speak, the very stones are mystical.
No spoken vows; let's be true loves instead.

In your heart's core you know your mind is fed
not by a woman's beauty but by her soul.
Marriage is more than four bare legs in bed.

In Paris, John MacBride and I have wed.
Now Gonne is gone, but Maud is your maid still.
Not flesh to flesh; we'll be true loves instead.
Marriage is more than four bare legs in bed.

FROM *A VOICE FROM THE HUMP*
1977

THE RETURN

Home was a flop. The woman flatulent
and fat, wedded to a half-filled bed.

Before my eyes, the bitch, pig from a pup,
heaved to her feet, grunted once, rolled dead.

Well on his way back to child, my father
imagined his arm could fling a spear.
It aroused a guffaw.

And my son, dear Goddess! a man
yet not a man, female infected, butt
of men's jibes, dreamer and dodger—phew!
unable to string a bow.

My beautiful people—palsied or gone
into shades. Their vulture sons,
pecking each other's eyes while I was off—
a phalanx of beaks within the eagle's nest.

Over the palace, moss everywhere.
Weary my brain, fevered by songs
of swallows following from the south.

      Now sail is set, the tiller steady.
      This time my own helmsman.

      Wind sputters, coughs, chokes on itself.
      Wonderful through the calm their voices flow.

      Scars from the ropes they'd braceleted my wrists
      and ankles with tell the whole story.

IXION

Love turned me to it. Groin,
groaning hub; head and arm
and legs, five flaring spokes;
self-rived, spread-eagled in
a swirling flame that lives
on flesh without consuming.

My sex, the source—a nub
of fire that feeds itself
and sparks those nerves radiant
to my extremities,
wherefrom a blazing arc
momently is flung.

Hell beyond burning is
the whipping of the brain,
the abrading of the pate
and palms and soles, the veer
away from where my gist.

I dream of roots and anchors
and all those frozen women
who support entablatures,
of heroes, kings and gods,
scarcely emergent from stone,
whose lives are frozen into
pediments and friezes.

GAWAIN

Dying at Dover, blood from the old wound,
got before Benwick of Lancelot,
bathing the brassard and bare forearms,
still gauntleted hands of his uncle,
the doomed king who held him, it came back:

That moment on Orkney's scarped coast,
alone, facing morning, when he drank in
not sunlight or heat but something more—
power strength force might main,
these merely words for what entered his blood,
made him seize a white rock his father-king Lot
and Agravain his knighted brother together
could not have budged, and heft it toward the sun,
directly overhead, feeding him like a mother,
then heave it seaward, out toward Dunnet Head,
where the whole vast southern kingdom lay.

Something warned him not to run home and tell;
but alarmed by the thump of his heart, the racing
of blood, he stretched out and slept on the sand,
dreaming himself the favorite hawk
of the kingliest lord of the southlands.

When he awoke the sun was low fire.
Although he could tell by mere feeling, he tried
a smaller rock and could not. The tide
reared high, like a stallion in battle. Inside
the jaws of water, wide before they closed,
illumined by a shaft of horizontal sunlight,
he saw three figures: a king mighty beyond
his father, who glanced askance in sorrow;

a gray-eyed queen, who smiled and nodded
an assent; a knight in bloodred armor, without
a helmet, who looked his anguished love.

The mouth of the wave snapped closed. He turned
toward home. Behind him, a man with a forked
white beard and pits for eyes that had been watching.

BEAUTY AND THE BEAST

i
No condescension shows, though she towers
above him as they talk while walking in.
Nor does he try to elevate himself;
his heels have not been lifted, hers are high.

He slides a chair—the perfect height to be
his partner—beneath her neat parenthesis.
Have they been sent here to torment me?

My guess is fifty years this Atlas shrunk
has been beneath the ball of flesh that willed
itself upon his back. From up here on a barstool,
the head of his that bears the face seems set
upon the table where he's seated, severed,
on a platter, like Baptist John's. A beauty,
maybe thirty, she'd tempt a chaste apostle.

ii
What's wrong with you?—YOU, not him.
You are the question mark, the crooked
exclamation point. Don't tell me you're
his traveling secretary, guaranteed a bedroom
of your own in this motel. His sister, are you,
returning together home to Daddy's funeral?
If you are for sale, I hope you wangled yourself
a juicy bonus. Might he be a hypnotist?

Come on, come on, you can't expect to travel
openly together and not provoke some questions.
The world's not blind or kind.

Too much of man erect, is that the story?
You're piqued by difference? Does oddity
amidst dull regularity excite you?
Ennui's victim, do you expose hypocrisy?

Could it be you're cold and slow, straitlaced,
high-minded and thus demand flesh flaw
to balance the elevation of the brain
and move you to the lower spheres of self?
His body—is it beautiful besides?
Do you idealize? Your imagination,
does it straighten out what's crooked?
Or is his second head a measure
of the manly size and power that you desire?
Have you an upright husband? a normal lover?
Are you two souls the way he is two heads?

Beneath it all, YOU have to be disfigured.
Does hide with matted hair cover you knee
to shoulder? Do iguanas, snakes and fish tattoo
your thighs and belly? Have your breasts
been surgeoned off, so I've been lusting on
an apparatus? Do scars deface your body?
Has your torso burned and healed
a hideous purple? Are you plastic-femme?
transvestite? changeling? Stowed in your luggage,
do you carry chains and whips, the Marquis' tools?

Tell me confidentially—does it yield
you extra pleasure? Dare you touch it? fondle it?
name it and coo to it? curl your flesh around it?
womb it between your breasts and navel? Does a voice
from in that hump cry, "Love me, love me!"
Is he your man because of not despite?

Anticipation, does it bring a dread? Do you have
to force a start, more painful every time?
Do you keep your eyelids clamped against it
during? Is your peculiar triumph transformation,
breeding from grotesquerie the purest love?

Together do you crowd the heels of demons?
Do angels weep for pity? What does the cosmos think?

iii
Sick, sick, sick, oh, I am sick from speculation
on the practices of lust, the art of love—
a Humpty-Dumpty on a barstool, lady.

PROEM

Supercharged, electrified, this atmosphere
(fraught with an aphrodisiac? infected with war?)
excites these trees to their roots; can't bear
it, these trees, can't without dancing—too much, too big breath for
them—dancing as though footloose, wilder, flinging more arms
than Siva, oh! they almost lose their heads
doing this dance before storm. How it alarms, alarms
us! Lights needed to relieve day's midnight within our sheds
blink astonished at their forebears: volcano winks
devilishly in heaven's open navel, flaming spume
from quenched sun (Cyclops' blinding?), fire through chinks
in space. Hear surf, rampant to land, in sky drums' boom.
Under a tidal wave sucked high by an invisible moon, the blood,
the eyes, the ears, the mind await the impending flood.

Rummage for My Brother

"What is it, what's going on?"
"Today is the day of the dead."

"What is the day of the dead?"
"Something new they've come up with—
bringing them back on buses one day each year."

"All of them?" "No, no, no, of course not.
Just those the living remember."

"How do you go about finding the one
you want to see?" "You simply have to look.
They haven't come up with a system yet."

    Eyes like stones, face after face as similar
    as fingerprints or fossils, their bodies
    strapped into seats, like babies in high chairs,
    not dressed in their best for burial but in what
    looked to be their everyday clothes before.

    As we worked our way up and down the aisle of bus
    after bus on that desert-like parking lot, we seekers
    kept our voices low and behaved politely.

    I had my eye out for that dog-eared sweater,
    the color of clay, he wore so fondly so long.

    A couple of times I thought I'd spotted him,
    but one turned out to be a child or a dwarf,
    the other, I think, an Asian woman.

A metallic voice gave us ten minutes warning,
as when a ship is about to depart. Somehow
all the buses got underway at the same instant.

So far as I've heard no one found anybody.
Maybe by next year they'll have worked out a system.

ONCE BY SEASIDE

For Joan

It began with that bracelet of seaweed
a tongue of ocean wrapped around
your ankle. You beachwalked, careless
of the ornament—or were you coy—
until a splash of tide unshackled you.

The herring gull we watched in quiet
terror was also involved: parachute
that never opened, dive-bomber,
shiverer of sea glaze with
his ice pick nose, again and again,
always to catapult up out of it.

Of course it came down to the night
on a sheet white as fresh-fallen snow—
yes, snow, in that tropical heat.

And we, we became two bodies inside
one skin, thrashing like a cat
and a snake in a sack, declining
at last to a single pulse, a tide
without land for its measure.

Back outside the self, each membraned
uniquely, how cut in half we felt.
Then even lust lay dead,

while the moon, framed by the window,
a stone honing the blade edge
of night, struck star-sparks
all the way down to the water.

ENTERING MADAME BOVARY

i
Hm…hm…[throat clearing]
to begin:
        My love and I trod…

What a howl! You never
trod anything.

        My love and I…

Come off it—
you never had a love.

        I…

No, you never.

        entered Emma Bovary once.

        nests in her armpits
        a mane down her belly
        shag on her gams
        and a pencil-line mustache

        she went at it so hard
        sweat pearled on every hair

        into her ear rather well
        chewed I whispered
        pretty words in Provençal
        I'd prepared for the occasion

her breathing when she came
made me fear she'd swallowed glue
her eyes lit up with jacks
of hearts and across her chest
flat as bad prose
RODOLPHE WAS HERE glowed crimson.

ii
Starting out of my latest dream,
I smothered my face in the pillow,
went blind and tasted
cloth and feathers.

Had Emma seen me then
she would have giggled.
"There lies a man with a pillow
for a head," she would have said.

So many years ago it was
I can't tell read from real
and has taken more time than most
are granted for shame to act.

iii
Did entering Madame Bovary
teach you anything about the dying arts?

Afraid not. The better the lay
the less one seems to learn that way.
And Emma was something,
despite some initial visual and tactile
disappointments. Take into account
her time came before *science appliqué*
made us mannequins. You know
those old perfumes failed in moments of crisis.

Well well well best lure
some inept whore inside your door
else grow greedier with age and rage.
At a certain time of life
you really should start learning how not
to live, must practice it like prayer.

All this is written in a letter
self-addressed instructions
for when to be opened printed
on the envelope which you'll find
right where you secreted it years ago
between two leaves
in the calendar of your life.

Ah, yes. That message from the past.
I'd forgotten. Emma gave
the best love after all.

ONE-WAY CONVERSATION WITH RANDALL JARRELL

i
You're not expecting, I know, pale horse,
pale rider to come clopping along the concrete,
damming traffic and provoking horns,
or ambling along the shoulder, lingering
to forage and chomp on clumps of grass
the highway crew had missed when mowing.
(Imagine, an *Erlkönig* on the berm.)
That was in once upon a time.

With it all you sit smiling: bearded like
a Nubian billy goat, black fedora cocked rakishly,
your wristwatch giving away time,
among milkweed, wild carrot, thistle on the hillside
of this boneyard above the freeway:
        SPEED LIMIT 65
        TRUCKS 55

ii
His style precludes a snorting diesel;
a hearse would broaden irony to farce;
an ambulance reduce it to mere prank—
besides, perhaps…nor either a preacher's car
or a chauffeur-driven Cadillac—God,
not the black of false humility
or crudely understated power.
No, no, your eye is qui vive
for a whore's-cheek red convertible,
roof furled. Perversity will provide
a paradisiacal day on earth.

One sign will be the Rorschach
on his parchment forehead: a chance splash
from the just-missing-its-target inkhorn
of the *Ehrwürdigen Vater Herrn* Martin Luther;
you'll read the mark of the Beast.
Another will be the blond lolling
beside him in after-coitus sleep,
a smile on her lips for the poet
who imagines he has had her. Of course
her forsythia hair will be blowing in the wind.

From the time you butted on this spot
he has been circling, bidingly:
"A dog in a tub on wheels who was the Morning Star."

And when, as it must, your eye recognizes,
when your will, as it will, staggers
among options, while your nerves tremble
from final disgust at being a being encaged,
sensing it's time he will whisper (so as not
to awaken his lady): "Now, no more terms."
Hearing above the hellhound howl
of the motors, you will answer:
"Signed and sealed for good neither
in ink nor blood but in my life."

iii
From that bank the drop is final as any from
temple's pinnacle, or plummet from the belly
of Plexiglas five miles up.
Your timing will be perfect:
before you can smack on the concrete
you will kiss off the grinning engine (you despise)
into the world (you love) of black swans.

FLOWER PYRE: WHEN ROETHKE DIED

On the backside of this cemetery,
unplotted land beyond gravestones,
concealed behind a wall of yew
and hemlock, smolders a heap
of withered greens and blossoms.

The fetor, stinging stink, smacks me
across the eyes, makes them water.

As if old Otto's greenhouse,
earth's clerestory, vast cocoon
of glass, where caterpillars turn
to butterflies—fumed like a city dump;

or that citadel on the hill, or in the sky,
after all these centuries of cantilevering
by our ablest architects of the abstract—
had turned to smoke.

Wire backbones of wreaths and sprays,
black snakes in white ashes, survive.

de BERRYMAN'S POSTHUMOUS DELUSIONS

"I can't bear any more."
—John Berryman

Enraged for love of Jesus and Walt Whitman,
he scraped his left cheek, chin, and wattles
clean as a turkey ready for the oven.
Then corked that half of his face.

That grand old clown John Berryman,
who wanted with all his heart to be a saint,
put on a pee-and-sweat-stained union suit.
From the trunk he stowed his precious gear in,
he plucked a parasol (for style,
not to keep him dry when he'd walk
beneath the water), went dancing tiptoe
toward the wire he knew was not across
our great divide, far north of Huck and Jim.

The silk-on-bamboo-wimpled single wing
that could not fly or float
he opened with a fillip.

A breathless quick descent, because his head
hung heavy on his heart. The parachute
wrong-sided out, up-cupped into a crocus,
its tassels exclamation points of horror.

Betting no net to save, no swooping arms
to bear him lest..., he cried "Mary Mother Mary"
all the way home, so plaintively you'd weep and cede
to him your place in Heaven if you had one.

AMONG THE AVOCADO TREES

Half blind, my mother in a rented room,
and I among the avocado trees;
my father in a madhouse, preaching doom,
and I at table with his enemies.

My brother picking pockets—a petty cheat,
and I a parasite upon a basking quean;
my sister selling sex along the street,
and I procuring love where toucans preen.

Before I headed south I passed the church:
no-trespass signs and padlocks sealed the doors;
the crooked finial—a pigeon perch;
blinding stained-glass windows—nailed on boards.

The adjoining manse had been converted by
the local American Legion to a post;
a cannon on the lawn advised the sky
it would brook no nonsense from the Holy Ghost.

Averting Heaven by the family fall
from grace, here under Capricorn at ease
I lie and listen to the toucans call
and dart among the avocado trees.

HITTING A PHEASANT ON THE PENNSYLVANIA TURNPIKE

Bird want? hen fear? maybe one
of those little earthquakes in the heart
that sends us scooting too? for I was driving,
restless between two points of rest.

Angling from the camouflage
of cornstalks, she arrows in the slit
where see begins, sheer motion;
quicker than think she expands to wings;
zaps against the windshield, shatterproof—
even our eyes we've armored like armadillos—
before my foot can jump from zoom
to stop; then bursts so big she's gone.

Fear flares cold nerves like circuited toaster wires.
Yet catching her crazy flutter on the concrete
in my rearview mirror, not dying raw but
dying's dumb show on a two-dimensional screen,
I've been conditioned man enough to boot
the sagging needle back to seventy-five.

Perhaps she was weighty with unborn birds,
sacrificing lift for life. Why not program
Pavlovian safety lessons for fledging pheasants?
breed in "need-speed gear," "superheft?"

The film runs out. By jerking my eye
from what's lying ahead to what my mirror
tells me I've left behind, I witness
her Technicolor finish by a trailing Buick,
green in a brown-feathered squall.

A nimble natural lawyer would evince
contributory negligence;
a Coke and Blackstone stickler force
dismissal on the technicality.

So, judge in me acquits me, with some wisdom:
guilt is a recognition we can't afford.
Our manufacture does the killing. Collisions
are time's complicities, history's physics.
Only an aggrandizing superego
would projectile causes from
the unfortuitous concourse of trajectories
that claimed one female pheasant life
along the Pennsylvania Turnpike back
to Dresden, Hiroshima, and momently to Hanoi.

ANATHEMA: FOR THE BOMBERS OF LAMBS

Birmingham, Alabama
Sunday, September 15, 1963

Light a liquid fire, Lord, within my mouth.

Their offering (burnt) on this Communion Day
resurrects the cannibal in me...
now could I drink cold blood,
devour inhuman human flesh.

For the sake of Jesus, lover of all kids
let no one simpering say,
"These did not die in vain."
And let no brother turn his other cheek,
no father dare forgive them,
for they knew what they did,
no mother yield another lamb for burning.

I pray each little black-charred bone tattoo
upon the membrane that their shriveled hearts
be stretched to, tenter-hooked across
the bottoms of their hollow skulls,
I pray a tide of boiling children's blood
seethe each naked nerve throughout their bodies.

This sacrifice burns up all love
it takes to make a human heaven,
rekindles in forebearing hearts
old fires of hell.

KAMIKAZE

Wait three days. Then inform
my father, gem merchant
of Hiroshima: "Early in the month
of the ripening plum, he answered
the call of the rising sun,
without sorrow."

To my mother convey this empty urn,
enameled with gulls on the wing,
from Shimabara in the south.
Speak no word, bow three times, retire.

Do not search for the girl
with oval hands and lustrous eyes.

Here in moonlight,
ahead of false dawn stands
the raven-winged plane
loaded with fire.

May it be a mother eagle, proud,
pregnant with predacious young.

Sometimes when you burn
the ceremonial tapers and scatter
incense before your sons,
remember, my friend, how we locked
fingers here...last human touch.

Not yet nineteen, I fly
to greet the sun and dive.

FULBRIGHT STUDENT

One Ahmed Salan, ex-FLN,
with two gold teeth,
with a Charlie Chaplin mustache,
and wistful smile, whose fingertips
look a little funny—

because his *compagnon*
Ben Ali Abbas will tell you
over beer, that "*un brigadier français
…tous les ongles…*"
(here Ben Ali pantomimes
the procedure while nodding
to assure you he speaks true history),

that Ahmed heard his sister's rape
"*par les paratroupes.*"
then escaped from les *bourreaux*
by leaping through a louver,
made it home to find his mother dead—
"*bombardement de représailles,*"

and later enjoyed "*le plaisir exquis*"
of capturing "*un seul et même brigadier*"
(here Ben Ali laughs and pounds the table)
in a midnight ambush near Laghouat
(now Ben Ali's right forefinger is dancing in
the air) and surgically yanked out "*unique ongle*"—
addresses me as "*monsieur le professeur.*"

"SOME SAY IN ICE"

—Robert Frost

Where field edge folds cleft drain rain came
rushing to rock edge of land and ran
over, gushed all day. Sun done, run
thickened, stiffened, oozed so slow flow
just inched over verge till chill still
deeper struck. On scarp's stone lip-tip drip
fixed, froze, closed sluice at last fast, past
running. Time can't outrace place; ice vise
holds, wins. So earth's blood-flood clots stops.

EMILY DICKINSON

A daughter among buttercups
whose father kept her fed
on dandelion drops
of wine and crumbs of bread.

Hers were absent lovers
dressed black as Bibles, all
too busy about their Father's
vast enterprise to call.

Each lightning flash she sinned
after exquisite pain…
naked to the lashing wind
and ravished by the rain.

She cadged from every sunrise
a kiss to seal election,
extorted from the butterflies
promised resurrection.

And set some crooked psalms
to syncopated airs
her neighbors heard as hymns
of praise and virgin prayers.

Now none of this would matter
more than shepherd's purses,
moss or tadpoles but that her
strangled cries, soft curses

were caught between the hills
in the river valley, where
we hear them echo still,
witching New England air.

MEDITATION

Nun on the rocks at Cape May Point

He heaved these rocks I sit on, black
against their gray, while saying morning beads
upon the sands of this peninsula.
He made it safe for us, bidding men
pile and jetty stones against the ocean's swell,
then mossed their sea side green to prove
His constant motion.

Such stones might vault a vast cathedral
for Our Lady—like St. Peter's rock—
a stronger stand against the breaking waves
than poor St. Agnes by the Sea,
our little clapboard chapel, duned
among mimosa wearing spraylike blows
and tall-stalked yucca, whose bell-shaped panicles
bloom like campaniles, our only carillon.

With lavish hand He salted all this water
and sowed it dense with fish—
eels that shoot electric; some with fins of green
that gleam at night and jaws that saw like bread knives;
others in far-off seas, they say, that even fly.

The moon, He made it round-faced, bald
and dull of light. And still it tames the sea
for Him—what wonder! He flings the waves
on rock and smashes them to spume.

One Sunday sunrise after morning prayers,
from this very jut of stones I think I saw
His face. Ocean was furrow-less, smooth as the sky,

and there beneath its blue transparent skin—
a floating smile, not awful or forbidding,
but as I imagine whales, with jolly eyes,
a huge brow, and little milk-white teeth.

I never told a single soul, not even our
Reverend Mother, and never saw or thought
I saw again. Since then I've slept
with surf sigh in my ear.

Lord, render me useful for Your flow
as is the moon, ardent to break myself
upon Your rock. And let grace wash
through me as soft as foam. You capped
all black the head of these white gulls—
so keep me hooded by Your marking will.

GULLS

When people go the hooded gulls come back
along these beaches where autumn tides lick slick
all summer scars and architectures.
East wind erases too. Then winter works
some drama into sandscapes: drifts, dunes, scoops,
hollows, shelves, breaks, and washouts. But always
smooth, for gulls leave only claw prints.
And in November gulls reclaim the shoreline.

At dawn their black and white bodies
pattern a patch of beach into a wobbly chessboard.
Swish! a prestidigitator whisks
a checked cloth off a table...gulls
go flapping up the sky and shaking out.

With glasses I zero in on a single bird:
banking, pumping stiff wings to brake,
hanging motionless, head dipped,
as if on wires slung from a vaulted roof,
plummeting to sudden purpose
hid within the sea in which he spears.
A beating of white wings, gray water thrashed,
a lifting spurt, and there he climbs the air
and skews away...aimless, it seems.

This very morning, swaddled in a woolpack mist,
a plane coming in on instruments
over Boston Bay noses into a squadron
of birds in wing-tipped sodality.
The gulls' dumb terror, scarce felt before
birds whole are sucked into turbines of
annihilation, hones the blade

of my imagination sharply enough
to make me feel the cruelty of it,
just as I also know the horror of the souls
aboard—a jump at the thud of collision
with the flock mass, catching the engines' choke,
hearing them wheeze on too much gull life,
lurching with the futile veer and spin, gasping
at the nosedive, to a bull's-eye in a placid sea.

FRATERNITY

Father's first son had his mother
snatched from him when he was seven.
He was told she'd gone to Heaven.
Heaven failed to send another.

His mother's hands as she was taken
clamped upon his heart and bruised it;
his slender shoot almost uprooted—
like a stripling apple shaken

loose from deep soil nourishment but
not felled. Married twice, he never
found his mother's living picture;
despite that, sired five daughters, fruit

for our father's family tree. No
learning fed his brain. No profession
could he follow—last bitter concession
granted at forty to his seven-year ego.

For his lost birthright my mother
tendered care that failed to make up.
Here in peccant rhyme a Jacob
love I tender my half-brother.

PRODIGAL SON

Church of childhood—how many bombs
have I plotted and planted, intending to wrack
your stones for years! Yet you stand intact
in mind: my father among palms,

crow-robed, charismatic with the Word,
declaring me guilty till beaten I
sin with the son who chose pigsty.
Unseen, all-seeing eye God lurks

in the intricacy of ceiling beams,
whose straight lines somehow conform to dome.
Hell brimstones in the boiler room,
where, dazzling with sweated blasphemes,

a man of shadows stokes and rakes
white fires, one "Deacon" Buell, born slave,
handsome with power despite an age
kid arithmetic couldn't calculate—

dark genesis of later lure
all underworlds would hold for me,
as the resolved geometry
of overheads has proved too pure.

No wonder—the in-between called life
stained by sun through glass Christ on cross,
was oak pew, serge suit, scant grape juice,
cubes of stale bread—I had to dive.

SELF-PORTRAIT ON MOUNT POCONO

My back is to the fire—birch and sappy
apple. Through an all-glass wall I scan
the heads of hemlock, spruce and fir
eye-level with this room. Beyond,
the valley dips from view to where
a sister slope ascends snow-blank,
upon which branches scrawl like
the lines of a Pieter Bruegel
landscape, desolate of hunters.

Dusk slithering in transmutes the pane
to a mirror that progressively sifts
the far world out. As night takes over,
reflected flames dance lambent on
one towering treetop, a prodigy—
Ascanius' head licked by the blaze
of Providence, Yahweh in a burning bush.

I, the witness, gathering as a dark
myself in the glass, depict scant dynasty,
little piety. Am projected rather,
when the beam you flick on from a lamp
in a corner crossing the flare of the fire,
locates a second center of composition
in the mirroring glass like Picasso's Jaime Sabartés:
                        eye wrenched toward nose,
                        nose splayed on cheek,
                        cheek gashed by slits of lips.

Such fractured physiognomy
illumines beyond x-ray, incises deeper
than the scalpel, as if the mountain sides

had shifted, opening fissures to
the gizzard of the world. And oh,
what creatures writhe in those crevasses!

It's mercy in your hand to draw
the drape, curtaining off the climax of
this chthonic drama. Then from behind,
your fingers touch to flesh again, restore
my broken face.

FROM *DEATH OF A CLOWN*
1964

DEATH OF A CLOWN

In memoriam Chico Marx

"Laughter is the surest test of the heart."
—Dostoyevsky, *A Raw Youth*

Goldoni, Cervantes, Sterne, and Ben and Will,
and all you nameless mimes and mountebanks,
you strolling jugglers, acrobats and harlequins
who had no place or master but haunted square
and fountain, market town and fair
serving the god whose worship is a laugh!

Among the anointed, clowns come first,
revered beyond a king or president,
more sacred still than martyr, saint or priest—
          I swear it by the thirty
          fingers of the Trinity—
for these the most are like to innocent children.

So this one haloed by yellow light,
underneath his cone of felt,
silver bell jingling
with every trip and catch,
each flick of finger, cock of head,
in somebody else's pants
and a blouse he never had grown into.

Oh, doubtless he once started out
on the road to manhood like the rout of us,
but sensing soon a crooked way
he wheeled around for good,
raced facing backward toward the child
he never quite had left...

skidding, stumbling, pitching, tumbling
along the low road to that theater
of perfect simpleness
where only clowns are all
the wise men, wizards, heroes, princes.

It's enough to make me wish that I were there
to hear it echo through the wings backstage...
"he's coming," "on his way"
from chops all new-fleshed now,
the laughing lips of Yorick,
Truffaldino and the limp-lanced knight,
of Mac who stole the Christ child
and he who's always slapped,
of Toby uncle to us everyone—

"Who? the bum with cane and derby
            and the wobbly feet?"
"the mutterer with a strawberry for a nose
            and roofless lid?"
"the brother with shoe polish on his lip
            and gargantuan cigar?"

"No, no, it's..."

And then to see him scoot onstage,
glissando down the keyboard of our spine,
plunk forefinger on the A
that opens a brand new play—
"I tell you a-what, boss..."

"And this one
my be-laughed son

in whom I am…"

Envoi
Speak to us, Chico, now more dumb
than even brother without a tongue
and pray through laughter we may come
into the immortal playhouse clowns call home.

CAROUSEL

In a cage out front, a chalk face, rouge
         bullseyed in each cheek.
         Her crooked fingers scoop
in coins, slide tickets underneath

the grille. Flanking the pavilion—
         a twelve-foot soldier
         greets the children.
He wears a faded coat and bandolier.

His fellow in welcome—a sad-faced clown
         in tattered motley.
         The wheezing sound
emitted by a steam calliope

sparkled maybe a hundred years
         ago. A dragon
         and reindeer,
hitched to a lusterless gilt wagon—

from fable and the North Pole?—
         once shone a brighter
         red, green, blue, and gold
than any rose, yew, azurite, or

polished ornament. They were wrought
         by the hand of an unknown
         artist who never thought
to put his name on what he'd carved and honed

for Del Monico Amusements
         in Philadelphia, Pa.,

in 1910.
These then eye-catchingly grand and gay,

animals are in a state of peel,
        like plane tree bark.
        Now the throbbing wheel
has stopped, a stranded Noah's ark.

Soon a clang warns fathers to retreat
        and surrender children to
        motion and wild beasts.
A skull-faced man sea-legs through

the herd. As he feels the wheel again beginning
        to turn, he collects
        tickets. From spinning
his life away, his balance is perfect.

A man with a brow that belongs on Mount Rushmore—
        no more than four feet tall,
        with feet planted on the floor
that does not turn—is watching all

that's going on in the whirling world denied
        him. With the stumps
        of his legs slightly astride
as if to straddle something, the hump

on his back makes him look like a little Hercules
        bearing the world's weight.
        Suddenly he sees
and fixes on a red-dressed chippy, her back as straight

as the tarnished pole her right hand slides
        up and down on while

         supporting the bronco she rides.
At a sailor astride a tiger she throws a smile.

He blows rings of smoke her way in reply.
         After they pass by him,
         they disappear and the eye
of the little giant picks up a child on a lion.

RACHEL ON LONG ISLAND SAND DUNE

I did not see her climb but caught
an instant against the sky
before she started down

of breeze feathering her wheat-brown hair
among fringes of stalk grass,
cousin to sea fronds,

as if she too had sprouted up from sand's belly—
or maybe a barrow of tawny Shinnecock dust
windy time and the sea conspired for hiding
the restless bones of her Celt and Saxon forebears.

Who but the child chosen to lead me into paradise
transfigured on a mountaintop among palm trees?

Then ski-like scudding down the combe
whose brown snow covered up her track,
seeming just to skim the hollow of the dune
as gulls scoop waves,

while I on the wet beach,
half-drowned beneath such cresting of my four-year daughter,
felt the backwash of all her downward days
from this apotheosis
till her bones are buried pearl,
pearl gnawed to sand,
suck all my fatherhood to sea.

A PRAYER FOR MY ANGUISHED FATHER

Let my father go, Lord
of my father, Who have screwed
Your thorn-crowned image in his fear-sick
brain and with knotted whips have hewed
and racked his nerves, the very cord
You lash him to himself with. Proved
is his manhood, Your divinity—
from his torment, Lord, set my father free.

Let my father go, Lord,
Whose breast gives no repose.
Unmiracle his boiling blood
to deep-well coolness; transpose
his dissonance to the final chord
of silence. From his barbed self remove,
Lord, him You crucify with love.

Let my father go, Lord,
Whose dying Son has nailed my father on
the shadow cross of self, and gored
his gentle side with his own weapon.
Close him as a formal word
seals a will. Lord, strap the millstone
to his strangling neck—I here provide
the counter love to call his tide.

ANCESTOR

In the center of the fire dance
      my forebear stands.
Warm comforts of the evening
      cannot melt him,
a startling steady shape
      in sheepskin cape.
His feet, two rag-swathed lumps,
      like rose bush stumps,
are burlapped against ice.
      With legs astride,
he confronts me accusingly
      across centuries
from the groundsel of his cote
      on a hardscrabble slope
I'll never find out where
      in gritstone Yorkshire.

His year and place tight-gripped
      by the same white fist
squeezing my spot on the globe
      and keeping me close
to a fire I complacently receive
      beyond a need...
while he, my father's father
      how many times, shivers
on the blade of indecision.

      A mother's sob of fear
and child's cough assault his ear.
      His desperate eye
is agonizingly tempted by
      the close-at-hand stand

of woods on the baron's land.
      Around his throat and wrists
he can feel the hempen twist.
      The black hood's a chill
on his father-driven will.
      With a block beneath his head
he'll imagine a sharp ax edge
      anxious for his throat.

The thought that the logs I tote
      to my living room,
already furnace-warm, and burn
      for cozy cheer
at the midnight of the year,
      when it's bitter cold and dark,
might have served to unfreeze hearts
      and blood, from whence will come
the line of my daughters and my sons,
      which thick and clotted,
reduced the days they were allotted—
      this thought pits my rhyme
against their cold-blooded time
      and the father who quailed
at the sight of the forbidding pale
      of arms across
the limit of his yeoman's croft
      (a scanty pantry), and at
each craftily muted footpad
      of the dutiful reeve.
How feeble is backward grief.

CORDS

The cord that grew inside her
served as a tube that kept
the me-to-be fed.

If it had strangled on
itself I would have been
one of the born dead.

When I outed the cord was snipped
and slipped into my mother's
feeble hand,

to be passed on to my father,
who pinned it on the sun
to get it tanned,

then knotted it securely
and tied it on a birch rod—
in lieu of pizzle.

After suffering seven levels
Dante could uncoil the rope
from around his middle,

while Jonathan Edwards saw
all of us as spiders
wriggling above

the Father's fiery yawn,
danglers on a slippery
filament of love.

I KNOW AN OLD CRONE

I know an old crone only found near places
where man-made things have begun to return
to the earth: rock foundations of ruined bridges;
timbers of ancient barns collapsed and rotted
away; harrows, plows and threshers abandoned
on the land and rusting to umber. And once inside
a plot a father long ago had cleared and tended
all his life, now almost field again, I watched
her kneel and scratch the bramble back from a slab
of wuthered stone, then peer as searching
out some legend gnawed on earth's tomb
by wind's tooth. Fisting one hand she looked
as though to knock, but slowly rose without
and scuffed her way across November fields.

BRUCE MITCHELL PAINTS

Limning a triangle
between navel and nipples
he cuts and flays,
stretches his skin on the easel
hair side down

for tones of gray
he snaps off rib ends
grinds bone to powder
spits to make magma

needing three splashes
of man's milk white
he ejaculates

five hunks of flesh
rough-carved with care
he slap-pastes on
as figures in
a lopsided circle

the precise purple
that will make
these musicians flesh
lives only in
the juice of heart—
he squeezes

and last jags blood
much dark now thick

from every shape
to every shape…

a jug band born
of Mitchell's guts.

No Line is Straight

No line we think or draw is straight
        upon this pellet
dropped from some wayward star—
        yet of such offal, lady,
whirling a wobbly loop
        around a dying light,
the miracle of you was born.

Only rounds are real; we know that
        our curving glance
can never rest on plumb—
        yet I would rather, lady,
than crumbling marble or crooked I beams
        inhabit your closing heart.

Look, suppose before our mother star
        freezes to dark
they wrench to square the circle—
        will earth then to Eden,
lady? pellet to pearl? will chaos luck
        another sun? sun
spin and hatch a second us?

THE ROLLERCOASTER

How teasingly it used to tug us
giggling
slowly up the long hill of lights,
up up up
around the backside of the moon
to one flat instant on a rounded top
where
holding breaths about to be sucked clean out of us—
our cotton-candied stomachs right behind—
we picked our star and grabbed,
as always our twelve-year arm
proved just a joint too short
and the brass ring—
could be the gold—
proffered the daring riders of the wooden palominos
never more than scraped our fingernail.

And how it used to send us
scooting down the darkness
underneath the moon
to a little breathless death
just a blink before the bottom:
then the thump,
the rush back in of life,
while across the ripples born out of the walloping wave,
we skimmed into the lighted shed
and stopped.

How dazzlingly like the rollercoaster's
are the climbs we make together
my lovely—
the tantalizing tugs,

the breathless instant
while lunging and clutching
for the star bubbling silver
forever unobtainable;
and how daringly like the rollercoaster's
are the leaps we make together,
my lovely—
the dying drop,
the bump at bottom,
the life welling back in against our will,
then the ski-ride over the little undulating humps—
now one swelling greater than the rest,
almost enough to snatch the breath again
but never quite—
and we're returned to the peopled world of lights.

When the minx comes along,
the slinking cat,
walking, stalking my way,
the midnight-black trull with emerald eyes
who sooner or later picks up
the scent of every last lover,
and tracks him down,
that's how I want to be taken,
my lovely—
a teasing tug to the top
by every muscle rippling in her body,
one last lunge toward those startling shoots
of light never to be seen again,
and then the skid,
the big breath-taking skid,
down the soft warm scoop of wonder-filled blackness
underneath the moon.

ANNIVERSARY PROCLAMATION

August 6

Let all coffin lids be made of glass.
Let graves be shallow, with no dirt on top.
Let corpses be buried naked, without rouge.

Let all cropped hair be stowed away in chests.
Let every paring from a nail be kept in a barrel.
Let each drop of spilled blood be stored in a vat.

Let every amputated member be preserved by freezing.
Let all excised organs, all cancers be displayed in showcases.
Let each miscarriage and stillbirth be pickled in a jar.

Let no particle of human flesh return to earth
nor fragment of human shape forfeit identity
nor any human creature claimed by death find rest

       until the old white god who crucified his son
       oh, how many times again upon a cross of fire
       that August morning at Hiroshima

       lops off his red right hand and lays it,
       an offering of peace, upon a shrine to man.

BOOKS FROM ETRUSCAN PRESS

The Disappearance of Seth | Kazim Ali

Toucans in the Arctic | Scott Coffel

Synergos | Roberto Manzano

Lies Will Take You Somewhere | Sheila Schwartz

Legible Heavens | H. L. Hix

A Poetics of Hiroshima | William Heyen

Saint Joe's Passion | J. D. Schraffenberger

American Fugue | Alexis Stamatis

Drift Ice | Jennifer Atkinson

The Widening | Carol Moldaw

Parallel Lives | Michael Lind

God Bless: A Political/Poetic Discourse | H. L. Hix

Chromatic | H. L. Hix (National Book Award finalist)

The Confessions of Doc Williams & Other Poems | William Heyen

Art into Life | Frederick R. Karl

Shadows of Houses | H. L. Hix

The White Horse: A Colombian Journey | Diane Thiel

Wild and Whirling Words: A Poetic Conversation | H. L. Hix

Shoah Train | William Heyen (National Book Award finalist)

Crow Man | Tom Bailey

As Easy As Lying: Essays on Poetry | H. L. Hix

Cinder | Bruce Bond

Free Concert: New and Selected Poems | Milton Kessler

September 11, 2001: American Writers Respond | William Heyen

etruscan press
www.etruscanpress.org

Etruscan Press books may be ordered from

Consortium Book Sales and Distribution
800-283-3572
www.cbsd.com

Small Press Distribution
800-869-7553
www.spdbooks.com